HAUNTED CANADA

The First Terrifying
Collection

HAUNTED CANADA

The First Terrifying Collection

PAT HANCOCK

illustrations by
Andrej Krystoforski and Kara-Anne Fraser

Scholastic Canada Ltd.
Toronto New York London Auckland Sydney
Mexico City New Delhi Hong Kong Buenos Aires

Scholastic Canada Ltd.
604 King Street West, Toronto, Ontario M5V 1E1, Canada

Scholastic Inc.
557 Broadway, New York, NY 10012, USA

Scholastic Australia Pty Limited
PO Box 579, Gosford, NSW 2250, Australia

Scholastic New Zealand Limited
Private Bag 94407, Botany, Manukau 2163, New Zealand

Scholastic Children's Books
Euston House, 24 Eversholt Street, London NW1 1DB, UK

www.scholastic.ca

Library and Archives Canada Cataloguing in Publication

Hancock, Pat
[Works. Selections]
Haunted Canada : the first terrifying collection / Pat Hancock ;
illustrated by Andrej Krystoforski and Kara-Anne Fraser.

Previously published separately as: Haunted Canada, Haunted
Canada 2, Haunted Canada 3.
ISBN 978-1-4431-6393-4 (softcover)

1. Ghosts--Canada--Juvenile literature. I. Hancock, Pat .
Haunted Canada. II. Hancock, Pat . Haunted Canada 2. III. Hancock,
Pat . Haunted Canada 3 IV. Krystoforski, Andrej, 1943-, illustrator
V. Fraser, Kara-Anne, illustrator VI. Title.

BF1472.C3H349 2018   j398.20971   C2018-901055-X

Cover credits:
Night: © Jag_cz/Shutterstock; Skull: © Joe Prachatree/Shutterstock.

8 7 6 5 4 3   Printed in Canada   119   21 22 23 24 25

To anyone who likes getting a scary thrill from reading spooky stories as much as I did when I was young.

FOREWORD

I love a good ghost story — the creepier, the better — full of cold drafts, ramshackle buildings and bumps in the night.

So when I was asked to write *Haunted Canada 4*, I was overjoyed . . . but I was also more than a little intimidated. I was very familiar with the first three books in Pat Hancock's bestselling series of true ghost stories and I was afraid that I wouldn't be able to uncover enough new material to write more than one or two new volumes. After all, Pat had already written about so many of the all-time scariest haunted Canadian locations and ghosts.

Take, for example, the Banff Springs Hotel in Alberta, with its resident ghost bride who is quite possibly the country's most well-known spirit. Or the tale of the Dungarvon Whooper, a murdered lumber camp cook whose nighttime wails make the bravest of people's blood run cold in Miramichi, New Brunswick. Or the burning ghost ship often spotted off the coast of the Northumberland Straight in P. E. I., complete with spectral people working frantically to put out the flames as the ship fades from view in thin air. Or the ghost of Captain Colin Swayze who haunts the Olde Angel Inn in what might be the most haunted town in the country, Niagara-on-the-Lake, Ontario. And all of these classic stories were published in the first volume!

But shortly after I began my own research I discovered that Canada, despite being such a young country, has no shortage of haunted locations. The fact that there are so many ghosts from coast to coast is fortunate for me as a writer, but perhaps less fortunate for Canadians who are easily scared.

The fact is Canada is a scary country. Really scary. Don't believe me? No matter. Pat Hancock is about to prove you dead wrong.

Joel A. Sutherland

INTRODUCTION

What sends chilly shivers down your spine? Hearing scratching on the window when you're home alone? Feeling something slither across your bare feet? Things like that can startle you, even scare you, but do they terrify you?

What about seeing a headless ghost racing across the park, or hearing howls and screeches coming from the empty car parked by the curb? Those would scare the pants off most of us, but maybe not if we just heard or read about them.

Spooky stories can scare us, but that's why we like them. We actually like the thrill of feeling frightened as long as the scary things aren't really happening, especially not to us.

But what if there really is a quivering cry for help coming from the sewer or blue lights drifting through the graveyard? Many people have reported terrifying tales like these. Here's your chance to read about some of them and experience those spine-tingling thrills you love. Just in case a few are too scary, you might want to make sure you keep the lights on.

Pat Hancock

THE APRIL GHOST

Oak Bay, Victoria, British Columbia

The young woman startled George Drysdale. He hadn't seen her coming but, suddenly, there she was, standing just a few metres away on the golf course, with her arms reaching out to him. Drysdale was frightened. He turned to get away from her, but there she was again, standing right in front of him. Frantic, Drysdale changed direction several times, but no matter which way he turned, she was there, facing him, dressed in white and looking terribly sad. Then, as suddenly as she'd appeared, she was gone.

Taking a few deep breaths to release the terror that had been building inside him, Drysdale headed back to where his sister and her friends were standing. They had seen him trying to avoid the woman in white, and were

1

wondering what had been going on. After he told them what had happened, they agreed that no human being could move as fast as she had. So who was the woman they had all seen? They could think of only one possible explanation for the eerie event on that moonlit spring night — George Drysdale of Toronto, visiting his sister in Victoria, had just met up with the April Ghost.

The ghost got her nickname because ever since 1936 people have reported seeing her in early spring — most often in April. She's also been dubbed the Golf Course Ghost because she's usually seen walking across the Royal Victoria Golf Course, near the ocean's edge. Every now and then she has also been spotted on a nearby road that winds along the coast. The ghostly young woman usually wears a long white dress that, to some, looks like an old-fashioned wedding dress. The dress's outlines are fuzzy, giving her a spooky, rather wispy look.

The April Ghost has been seen moving about on the golf course as early as 5 p.m., but she seems to prefer visiting late in the evening — an hour or two before midnight. Her scariest appearances have her materializing suddenly, rushing up to someone as if looking for help or warning the person about some nearby danger and then melting into thin air. George Drysdale seems to have met her doing this over and over again.

But why would such a restless spirit haunt a calm, quiet place like a golf course? Perhaps the answer to that question may be found in the golf course's past, when the body of a woman was found there, buried in a sand trap. The dead woman was identified as a nurse named Doris Gravelin, and she had been brutally strangled. She had last been seen walking on the golf course with her husband, Victor, the evening before she was killed.

Doris and Victor were known to have fought a lot, and were not living together at the time of her death. Right from the start, police saw Victor as their prime suspect, but they never got to charge him with his wife's murder. While they were building a case against him, he drowned himself in the waters of Oak Bay, just along the shore by the golf course. Not long after, reports started coming in about a mysterious woman in white haunting the area.

Local believers say Doris must be the April Ghost. But is she running to people for help or warning them to stay away from a place where such terrible things happened? Both theories are popular, and there is even a third idea about what she's up to. According to some, it's usually couples who aren't married that report seeing her as George Drysdale did: rushing forward with outstretched arms and then disappearing. Perhaps she is trying to warn couples about the dangers of a bad marriage, like her own.

THE NiGHTMARE KNOTS

Montreal, Quebec

The year was 1929. The place was a house in Montreal on Rue Ste. Famille, just west of Boulevard St. Laurent and north of de Maisonneuve. To passersby, the house looked perfectly normal. There was no outward sign of the bizarre things going on inside, and the people that lived there were too afraid to tell anyone about their troubles.

Eventually a reporter learned what was happening on Rue Ste. Famille, but even then the adults in the house insisted he not include their names when his story was published. After all, they were being troubled by knots. Who would believe that knots could be scary?

The knots started to appear without any warning that there was a troubling presence in the house. Knotted sleeves in sweaters were a nuisance, but could have been a practical joke — even if the prankster refused to own up to his or her handiwork. The knots in the towels were annoying; the ones in the curtains even more so, because they left behind unattractive wrinkles that had to be ironed out. Soon small, tightly twisted knots were appearing everywhere in the house — in sheets, pillowcases, tablecloths and dishtowels, in socks, shirts, dresses and trousers.

The parents were frantic. They spied on their children, hoping to catch a young culprit in the act. They even found themselves spying on each other. When they were absolutely certain that no family member was tying the knots, they did the only thing they could think of to bring them peace. They asked two priests to come and bless the house. But despite the priests' efforts, the knots continued to appear. Finally, feeling desperate, the family called in the police.

The police were intrigued with the mystery. They carefully examined the many knotted items, questioned everyone in turn and searched the house thoroughly from top to bottom. While searching the basement, one officer detected an unpleasant odour of decay. Could it be, he wondered, that a body had been buried there, and the dead person's ghost was tying the knots so that someone would look for the body? Armed with shovels and pick-axes, the police poked about and dug up much of the basement, but found no evidence of a crime or a corpse.

Another police officer came up with an experiment to make sure no human was tying the knots. Officers left several handkerchiefs in one of the rooms, and locked and sealed the door behind them. When they broke the seal and unlocked the door the next morning, they were amazed to find the cloth squares twisted into tiny knots.

Next they decided to have every member of the family tie knots in several different items. Then they studied all the knots carefully. What they learned surprised them. The knots appearing throughout the house looked just like those tied by the youngest child. The police figured she must have been tying the knots in some sort of trance-like state, with no memory in her conscious mind of what she was doing. From their point of view, the case was finally closed. Curiously enough, the knots stopped appearing not long after their investigation ended.

But the parents were never convinced that the police had truly solved the mystery. From their point of view, their young daughter couldn't possibly have been the phantom knotter without their knowing it, and the police should have felt the same way. They were the ones who had sealed the room with the handkerchiefs in it. And they were the ones who had found the seal still intact the next morning, with the handkerchiefs all tied up inside.

Did a ghostly double of the young girl haunt the house for those few months in 1929? It seems a little hard to believe. But that explanation makes at least as much sense as the one put forward by the police, especially in light of the results of their own experiment. According to them, no human, not even a child, could have entered that sealed room.

OTHERWORLDLY ENCORE

Winnipeg, Manitoba

Laurence Irving was the son of Sir Henry Irving, a famous Victorian actor. Sir Henry was the first actor ever to be honoured with a knighthood. Like his father, Laurence was also a talented stage performer. So was Laurence's wife, Mabel Hackney. After starring in a play in Winnipeg in May 1914, the popular British couple took the train east to Quebec. There they boarded the ocean liner *Empress of Ireland* to return home to England.

On the evening of May 29, while the *Empress of Ireland* was still in the St. Lawrence River, it was rammed by a Norwegian ship. In just 14 minutes the *Empress* sank, claiming the lives of 1014 passengers and crew. Laurence Irving and Mabel Hackney were the two most famous passengers to die so tragically that night.

7

There are those who say the ghosts of Irving and Hackney never left Canada, but stayed on where the actors had given their last performances — at the Walker Theatre in Winnipeg. Built in 1906, the theatre was

Actors Mabel Hackney and Laurence Irving

renamed after singer Burton Cummings in 2002. It has more than 1600 seats and is home to many performing arts events. It is also a place where creepy things happen; things that some people blame on the spirits of the two famous actors.

Hearing applause in a theatre isn't scary; it's expected. But what if it's coming from rows of empty seats? That's been reported at the theatre. So has the opening and closing of heavy steel doors. Who was clapping? Who was pushing and pulling on the doors? Who kept shutting dressing room doors after the night watchman made sure they were open? Are Irving and Hackney moving around the theatre, still giving encores so many years after their final bows?

One security guard wouldn't find the idea of ghostly actors at the Burton Cummings Theatre such a far-fetched idea. After all, it was he who finally wedged the dressing room doors open, only to find the wedges kicked out and the doors closed the next time he checked the halls. He's also the one who reported that his normally friendly, lively dogs would behave quite strangely when making nightly rounds with him. Instead of straining to get ahead of him, they would often press up against his legs as if frightened by something. They would also suddenly start barking for no obvious reason.

Maybe the dogs could hear or sense what an investigative reporter's tape recorder picked up one night, when human ears detected nothing. Although the theatre was empty, a recorder left running for a couple of hours captured sounds of footsteps, hammering and even a few whispers. One of the whispers sounded very much like someone saying, "Please . . ."

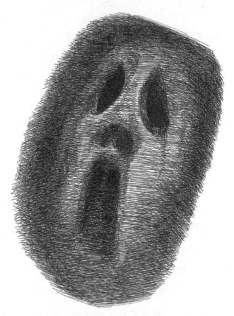

THE MOTORCYCLE GHOST

Lake Scugog, Ontario

Scugog Island is a big island in Lake Scugog about 65 kilometres northeast of Toronto. On the island is a road that ends at a farmer's field. It's been officially named Ghost Road. A romantic spot, especially on a moonlit night, it has quite a reputation as a lovers' lane. But many young people who find their way there aren't really looking for privacy. They know they're likely to find quite a few cars at the end of Ghost Road, all with their lights off and all parked facing south. It's a strange scene, and between 11 p.m. and 2 a.m. it often gets stranger. That's when the ghostly white light usually appears.

More often than not, those waiting to see the light aren't disappointed. It has been appearing for over four decades, on at least 200 nights of the year. It's more likely to materialize in October and November, the months on either side of Halloween. At first the light appears off in the distance, towards the south end of the field. Over the next minute or so it bounces along just above the ground, moving in a northeast direction, coming closer and closer to anyone waiting to see it. Then, just before the light disappears, there's a brief flash of a small red light trailing behind it. Not everyone sees the red light, but some people have seen the white light as many as ten times in one night. It's not unusual for it to appear at least twice in the same evening.

For years now people have tried to find the source of the light. Police have investigated it; traffic inspectors have checked it out. Even airport officials have looked into a possible cause. Some daring young men have run after it on foot; others have foolishly tried chasing it down in their cars. Officially, the cause of the light remains a mystery.

But according to local lore, the unofficial explanation is to be found in a tragic tale of death. One version of the story has the accident happening back in the 1950s to a teenager named Sweeney. A more specific account says it happened in 1963 to an unnamed youth. Both stories tell of a carefree young man riding his motorcycle across the fields late at night. In the darkness he didn't see the fence wire, and so, when he hit it at top speed, he was decapitated.

Ever since then people have seen the light. And ever since then, night after night, young people gather to wait for the appearance of Sweeney, headless, forever racing his motorcycle across the field at the end of Ghost Road.

THE BLOODSTAIN IN THE ATTIC

Calgary, Alberta

Deane House was built in 1906 for Richard Burton Deane, Fort Calgary's North West Mounted Police Superintendent. Over the years the stately house has also served as a railway agent's home, a boarding house, and a gallery and studio space for local artists. But during the late 1980s and early 1990s, many people weren't too comfortable staying at Deane House. And who could blame them? Most of us wouldn't want to stick around a place full of mysterious noises, where chairs and dishes might suddenly start flying around and smashing to the ground.

But why were such spooky things happening at Deane House? During the time that the building was a rundown, neglected rooming house, several of its tenants were brutally murdered, and others committed suicide. Could it be that the ghosts of these unfortunate souls were haunting the place? Some people thought so.

A religious ceremony performed at the house in the mid-1990s seemed to have a calming effect. Deane House was renovated again and over the years has been transformed into a cozy restaurant with a great view of the Elbow River. But it looks as if hungry diners aren't the only ones who find the atmosphere there welcoming. According to several eyewitnesses, some very strange things still happen at Deane House; things that suggest otherworldly spirits may still be hanging around.

First there's the matter of the mysterious woman in white. She appears in the attic every now and then. Is she the ghost of a former boarder whose husband stabbed her and then killed himself? Robert Jensen, a Deane House supervisor, thinks she could be. That might also explain the red patch in the attic. Jensen says it looks very much like a bloodstain, adding that it changes colour — from fresh-blood red to dried-blood brown — depending on what time of the year it is.

Then there are the phantoms that open and close doors and windows, toss small items into the air and grab and hide things when you turn away for a second. Jensen thinks the ghosts of Deane House do stuff like this when they're bored. Apparently boredom has also driven them to make an antique phone that no longer works start ringing as if it were new. And invisible hands have been known to poke at the keys on an old typewriter on display in a small den.

Some people think tales of ghosts at Deane House are simply that — tall tales intended to attract more customers to the restaurant. But when one lunch guest made that point to a staff member, her teacup started drifting up above the table. The woman accused staff of playing a trick on her, but, try as she might, she couldn't figure out how they could have pulled it off.

One waitress felt so uncomfortable working there that she quit after just a few months. Smelling pipe tobacco and hearing laughter in empty rooms made her nervous, but staying around to lock up at the end of the day was even spookier. When she had to turn off the lights on the upper floor and walk downstairs, she felt as if she were being followed so closely that she could feel someone's breath on her neck. After being left to lock up a few times, she decided it was time to start job-hunting again.

Robert Jensen admits that the ghostly goings-on gave him the jitters at first too. But rather than being scared off, he says "Good morning, ghosties" when he comes to work, and he ends each day with an equally friendly good-night to the phantoms of Deane House.

Deane House

GHOSTS IN THE RIGGING

Mahone Bay, Nova Scotia

Privateering was a dangerous way to make a living, but it could also be a quick way to make a fortune. When countries were at war, their governments would give permission to some private ship owners to attack enemy merchant ships and claim any loot they found for themselves. Doing this allowed the navy to spend more time fighting sea battles, and it robbed the enemy of needed supplies carried by the merchant ships.

During the War of 1812 several American privateers chased down British ships sailing along the southeastern coast of Nova Scotia. But on June 27, 1813, one of those American ships, the *Young Teazer*, became the hunted instead of the hunter.

A British navy warship chased the *Young Teazer* into

Mahone Bay west of Halifax. A British deserter aboard the *Young Teazer*, realizing that his ship was trapped and about to be boarded by British officers, made a desperate move. Knowing that if they found him he'd be hanged, he threw a lit torch into the ship's supply of gunpowder.

The fiery explosion that followed blew apart the *Young Teazer* and killed many of the crew. Some of the sailors were buried in the nearby town of Chester, and parts of the ship not destroyed by fire were hauled ashore to be used as building materials.

About a year later, a ghost ship made its first of many appearances near Chester in Mahone Bay.

Ever since then, hundreds of people have seen a burning ship out on the bay. Some of them were in their own boats when the ship appeared out of nowhere. At times it seemed to be heading right for them, and they were terrified that it was going to run them down. At the last second, it vanished into thin air. Sometimes it passes so close to the shore that people on the beach can see the sailors up in the rigging. In most cases the ship appears to be on fire, which is why so many people believe it is the ghost of the *Young Teazer*. Over the years, some people have even reported hearing the tortured cries of the men who have been trying to escape the burning ship for more than a century.

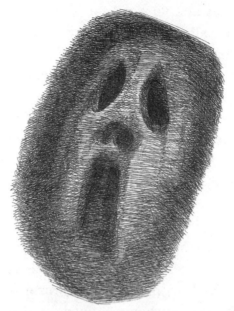

LAKESIDE HORROR

Red Deer Point, Manitoba

It was the second week of March 1898. Five men — three Canadians and two Norwegians — had taken the train from Winnipeg to Winnipegosis Station. From there they had travelled by wagon to an isolated fishing camp on Lake Winnipegosis, near Red Deer Point. The camp's buildings were sturdily built and well-stocked with everything needed to make the men's stay a pleasant one. When they arrived, they were looking forward to a week or two of good company and great fishing. By Wednesday, March 9, they were beginning to think they should never have left Winnipeg.

Details of what happened became public when one of the men — a Mr. A.C. O'Beirne — sent a letter from the camp to the *Winnipeg Free Press*. Strange as the story seemed, the newspaper's editor decided to print it on March 17. After all, Mr. O'Beirne was well known in the community. He wasn't the kind of person to make up such a terrifying tale and claim it to be true.

According to O'Beirne, a loud scratching sound at a window on Wednesday evening was the first sign of some otherworldly force at work. That noise, together with pipes banging and the sound of something being dragged across the roof, started around 9 p.m. and kept the men awake until about midnight. And, as O'Beirne pointed out in his letter, "We could find nothing to account for these noises, though we did our best to do so."

On Thursday evening, a small bell started ringing. At first its tinkling seemed to be coming from the stable. After a while it seemed to move closer to the main building and then, right inside. Again, the men couldn't find the source of the ringing. Worse still, the scratching, banging and dragging started up too.

Those spooky noises weren't all that invaded the men's peace and quiet Friday night. That evening, tin dishes were flung off the shelves onto the floor, and boots and overshoes were whipped across the room. A few men from a nearby lumber camp were on hand that night, and they too witnessed the nightmarish sights and sounds.

O'Beirne's description of what happened Saturday is chilling. As well as the scratching, banging, dragging and ringing, O'Beirne told of a heavy iron stove lid being lifted and thrown on the floor, a ladle being tossed out of a pot and then put back in it, and one man's hat flying off a nail onto his head. The paper O'Beirne was writing on was snatched out from under his hand, and the table he was working at began to shake.

Around 10:30 p.m., the lamp blew out and, as O'Beirne

put it, "Pandemonium let loose. Everything in the camp seemed to be on the move. The blows on the window were delivered with apparently sledgehammer force, the stoves rattled and shook . . . and there was also a loud knocking at the door. This happened three times, and then gradually the disturbances became less and ceased as usual shortly before midnight."

O'Beirne ended his letter with a plea to readers to come up with some sort of reasonable explanation for what happened at the fishing camp. But the best explanation anyone could offer was that the camp had been haunted by a poltergeist.

Poltergeist comes from two German words — *poltern*, meaning "to knock," and *Geist*, which means "spirit." The term poltergeist refers to mischievous, sometimes mean, spirits that do things like make strange noises, shake and rattle furniture and windows, snatch and grab small items and send objects flying around a room. Poltergeists are usually active at night, and after a few days or weeks, they seem to stop what they're doing as suddenly as they started.

That certainly sounds like what happened on Lake Winnipegosis back in March of 1898. Still, would O'Beirne have thought poltergeist haunting was a reasonable explanation for what he and his fishing companions saw and heard? Who knows. But simply naming the type of spirit that may have haunted the camp wouldn't have made the experience any less terrifying for the men who suffered through it. Poltergeist or not — it had scared the wits out of them.

THE HAUNTED HOTEL

Banff, Alberta

Each year thousands of tourists from around the world travel to Banff, Alberta, attracted by its incredible natural beauty. And those who can afford to often stay at the luxurious Banff Springs Hotel. Built high in the Rockies in the 1880s, the hotel offers spectacular views of the snow-capped mountains and the Bow River valley. Outside it looks like an old Scottish castle. Inside it provides guests with every possible comfort. Many people like the hotel so much they say they wish they didn't have to leave. Some people believe that a few individuals have decided to stay on forever, even in death.

Over the years there have been several reports of ghostly sightings at the "castle in the Rockies." A mysterious bartender is said to occasionally appear in the bar to tell patrons who've had too much to drink they should call it a night and go to bed. There have also been tales of a wandering bagpiper who might be looking for what he's lost — namely his head. But most reports about seeing phantoms involve two ghosts in particular.

The first is said to be a regular at the hotel. He's even been given a name — Sam. While Sam seems to prefer hanging around on the hotel's ninth floor, he's been spotted in many different areas of the building. Guests who claim to have met up with Sam report seeing a man wearing an old-fashioned bellhop's uniform. But Sam doesn't just look like a bellhop; he acts like one too. Always polite and helpful, he's carried bags for guests and opened doors for a few who have locked themselves out of their rooms. But as soon as someone tries to chat with him or offer him a tip for his services, he leaves so quickly it's as if he disappeared.

Guests' descriptions of Sam and his uniform suggest he might be a bellhop who worked at the hotel more than 70 years ago, but no one knows for sure. One thing is certain, though — there's no real person who looks like Sam working at the hotel.

The second phantom that several people have seen drifting around the hotel is an unnamed woman wearing a flowing white gown. Hers is a tragic story. It's said that she is the ghost of a beautiful young bride whose family had booked the grand ballroom for a magnificent wedding party. As she started walking down the marble staircase with her new husband to join their guests, she tripped on the long train of her dress. Another version of the story says her gown brushed against candles on the stairs and caught fire, and she stumbled as she whirled around to stamp out the flames. Either way, her husband tried desperately to stop her from falling, but she broke her neck as she tumbled down the stairs and fell dead on the floor below.

Does the spirit of that young bride really haunt the hotel where she died? Banff Springs representatives say no, adding that the sad tale was started as a public relations prank decades ago. But over the years a few people have mentioned feeling an icy breeze slip past them as they walked down the marble staircase. Others claim to have caught a passing glimpse of a young woman in white coming down the stairs. And still others say that they've seen, just for an instant, a vision of a beautiful girl in a flowing white dress, waltzing alone across the grand ballroom floor.

Banff Springs Hotel

THE GHOST TRAPPER

Eastern Labrador,
Newfoundland and Labrador

It's said that some ghostly spirits are doomed to wander the earth forever, unable to find peace after death because of the terrible things they did while they were alive. That notion is often put forward to explain the haunting appearances of the Ghost Trapper of Labrador. Also known as Smoker, the mysterious trapper is usually identified as Esau Dillingham, a Newfoundlander who moved to mainland Labrador in the early 1900s.

He'd come in search of better hunting grounds, but after running his new trap lines for a year or so, Dillingham decided there had to be an easier way to make a living. He became a bootlegger and cooked up his illegal alcohol in a backwoods still. Then he peddled it around to willing and eager buyers. It was disgusting tasting stuff, nicknamed smoke by the locals, who started calling its maker Smoker. It was also a potent brew; so much so that it was often poisonous. More than a few men went crazy drinking the stuff. For some, it was lethal.

Eventually the RCMP caught up with Smoker, but he didn't change his ways. After spending a year in jail in St. John's, he went right back to running a still and selling his illegal booze. But he was better at it this time. He rounded up a team of snow-white dogs, painted his wooden sled white and made himself a parka and pants from white furs and skins.

The camouflage worked. As Dillingham roamed the coast of Labrador selling his deadly drink, he blended in perfectly with the snowy drifts and blizzard-driven whiteouts. The police couldn't catch him and the money rolled in. But a lot of good it did him. Smoker had taken to drinking his own smoke.

As the madness crept in, Smoker lost control. One version of the story has him arrested in 1920 for murdering a customer, and then falling in his jail cell and breaking his back. Another version has him staggering around on a fish-drying rack, or flake, and breaking his back in a fall from the flake. Either way, a fall killed him. But just before he died, his head filling with searing visions of hellish torment, he prayed to be spared eternal punishment. He prayed for the chance to keep driving his dog team after death so he could make up for all the bad things he had done.

After Smoker's death, a few people reported hearing the sounds of a dog team being urged on by its driver. When they looked outside, they saw nothing and there were no sled or dog tracks in the snow. Others reported seeing a mysterious sledder dressed in white racing across the snow-covered landscape. Both types of appearances seemed to occur just before a severe storm blew in. Was it Smoker's ghost, trying to warn people to take shelter from an approaching blizzard? Some people thought so.

There are other stories of the ghostly trapper doing good deeds. One involves a lost hunter who was guided to safety during a blustery storm by a large man dressed all in white. Another involves two RCMP officers on patrol in Labrador in 1949. Supposedly the Mounties, lost in a blizzard, were dangerously close to freezing to death. With barely enough strength left to urge on their husky dogs, the men despaired of ever making it back to headquarters. Suddenly, another man appeared in the distance. He was dressed all in white and he was driving a team of 14 white dogs pulling a white sled. The Mounties decided to follow him.

Two agonizing hours later, almost blinded by snow and ready to drop with exhaustion, the Mounties came upon a cabin where some trappers had taken shelter from the storm. They staggered inside, assuming their rescuer had done the same because they had lost sight of him out-doors. But he wasn't there, and the trappers told them he never would be. They told the Mounties they had been saved by Smoker, a murderer whom other lawmen had brought to justice nearly 30 years earlier.

Was that dramatic rescue one more example of the Ghost Trapper of Labrador keeping his deathbed promise to do good in the afterlife? Maybe, but there are problems with the Ghost Trapper story. For one thing, the Newfoundland Rangers patrolled Labrador from 1935 to 1950. The Royal Canadian Mounted Police didn't assume law enforcement duties in Newfoundland and Labrador until 1950, a year after Newfoundland joined Confederation.

Moreover, before 1935 no one force was responsible for policing most of Labrador. It seems highly unlikely that members of the Newfoundland Constabulary would have crossed the Strait of Belle Isle to chase a bootlegger all over the mainland during winter storms and drag him back to a St. John's jail. And if Smoker had murdered someone, wouldn't there be an official record of that crime? You would think so.

So what part, if any, of the Ghost Trapper story is fact? It's hard to say. What does seem to be true is that every now and then, someone caught a glimpse of a mysterious figure dressed in white, driving a team of white dogs that pulled a white wooden sled. And any unexplained events that happened next have only fed the legend of the ghostly bootlegger who seeks redemption.

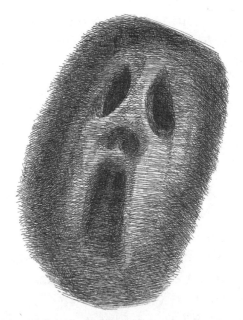

THAT REBEL SPIRIT

Toronto, Ontario

William Lyon Mackenzie was a crusading newspaper editor and publisher, a fiery provincial politician, Toronto's first mayor and leader of the Rebellion of 1837 in Upper Canada (now Ontario). That's an impressive list of accomplishments, and one that would probably have brought most people not only fame, but fortune too. But Mackenzie was an honest man. He never took bribes and he never accepted government money for jobs he didn't do. All his life he fought that sort of corruption, and all his life he struggled to make ends meet.

After the government crushed the rebellion, Mackenzie had to escape to the United States to avoid imprisonment or, worse still, a date with the gallows. During the next 12 years in exile, he tried to make enough money to care for his family by writing, taking odd jobs and publishing a few small newspapers. In 1849, when he was pardoned and allowed to return to Canada, he came back to Toronto.

Mackenzie went right back to attacking government corruption as both a newspaper publisher and an elected politician. However, he wasn't nearly as popular as he had been in the 1830s and, over the years, he found it harder and harder to survive, both politically and financially. In 1858, tired, in poor health and in debt, he resigned from the legislative assembly of Upper Canada. Faithful friends, who hadn't forgotten how hard he had fought for just causes, raised enough money to provide him and his family with a furnished house. Mackenzie died there three years later, in 1861.

The house, at 82 Bond Street, was rescued from the wrecker's ball in 1936 and was gradually restored to look as it did when Mackenzie lived in it. It's now a museum with many of his belongings on display. There's even a printing press like the one he used set up in the basement. It's still in working condition, but back in 1960, Mr. and Mrs. Alex Dobban, live-in caretakers at the house, had every reason to wish it weren't. Every now and then, when they were alone in the place, they would hear the press rumbling away in the basement. They also heard footsteps pacing around the house and the piano playing all on its own. The Dobbans moved out after only a few months of this, and from then on the building's caretakers lived outside of the house.

But the incidents that made the Dobbans nervous were minor compared to what had happened to the caretaking couple that came before them. Mr. and Mrs. Charles Edmunds lived in a third-floor apartment of Mackenzie House from 1956 to 1960. It was only four years, but for

Mrs. Edmunds, her time there was almost more than she could bear. She learned to put up with the mysterious footsteps, and wasn't too frightened by the rumbling noises in the basement and the rocking chair that moved back and forth as if there were someone in it. But she found the apparitions to be very disturbing.

Several times she caught sight of a long-haired woman in an old-fashioned dress wandering the halls. Occasionally she encountered a short, bald man wearing a nineteenth-century style jacket. Her description of the man was eerily similar to Mackenzie's appearance, except for his baldness. But the rebel leader's famed red hair was actually the product of a skilled wigmaker. Mackenzie had turned to wigs when he lost most of his hair, but maybe he felt comfortable enough at home to leave his wig on the dressing table, and his spirit felt the same way.

But it was a second long-haired woman who truly terrified Mrs. Edmunds. The first time she appeared, Mrs. Edmunds was in bed. She'd been asleep for a couple of hours when a touch on her shoulder woke her up. She looked up to find a woman looming above her. The woman appeared to be standing between the wall and the headboard — a space too narrow for any human being to fit. Her long brown hair dangled down near Mrs. Edmunds' pillow. Then suddenly, the woman disappeared.

The ghostly apparition stayed away for a year, but when she reappeared, she did so in a most dramatic fashion. Once again she woke up Mrs. Edmunds, hovering over her from above the headboard. But this time, before she faded away, she reached down and hit Mrs. Edmunds in the face. Mr. Edmunds comforted his hysterical wife and coaxed her back to sleep by saying she'd just had a bad dream. But Mrs. Edmunds knew better. When she

Mackenzie House

woke up the next morning, one side of her face was sore, and when she looked in the mirror she saw why. Her eye was red with broken blood vessels, and a dark bruise was forming around it.

After the Dobbans moved out in 1960, a minister performed a religious service to drive the otherworldly spirits from the house. After that the haunting incidents seemed to stop. Some people said reports of ghostly visitations had been invented to attract visitors to the historical museum. But no one could convince Mrs. Edmunds that what had happened to her had just been a publicity stunt. Her black eye was all the proof she needed that something spooky and strange had been going on at Mackenzie House, something she was very relieved to be done with when she and her husband moved out.

THINGS THAT GO BUMP IN THE NIGHT

Kenosee Lake, Saskatchewan

Nestled on the southeastern edge of Moose Mountain Provincial Park, Kenosee Lake is a popular summer resort with impressive scenery, good fishing and great camp-sites. And for those who are looking for some otherworldly entertainment, it's also said to have a haunted nightclub.

For more than ten years now, folks have been talking about the spooky things that happened at the Moosehead Inn, a former dance hall that was once a favourite hang-out for teenagers.

In 1990, Estevan resident Dale Orsted bought the inn and decided to fix it up a little. But he'd only had the place a few months when he started noticing that things like ashtrays, cutlery, glasses and figurines were disappearing at an unusual rate.

At first Orsted thought a few customers or staff members might be suffering from a bad case of sticky fingers. But the missing items started showing up again, often in the weirdest places. Then the loud noises started. Banging on the locked front door, thumping on the floors overhead — the racket could last for hours. Frustrated and frightened, Orsted called the police, but they couldn't figure out who or what was causing it.

In 1992, things went from bad to worse. One night, after the last customers had left, Orsted and a friend began ripping up some smelly old carpeting. Almost immediately the noises started up again, this time louder than ever. Sounds of large metal objects crashing into each other were so loud they nearly shattered the windowpanes.

The ear-splitting, nerve-jarring clanging and banging went on all week, night after night, until all the new carpeting was installed. Until then, Orsted had laughed whenever anyone suggested his place might be haunted. After that harrowing week, he found himself — against his better judgment — agreeing with them.

The presence of a ghost could also explain other things that started happening at the Moosehead. The lights flickered several times a night, the dishwasher turned itself on and off, a pail flew across the dance floor, and locked security doors suddenly crashed open and slammed shut. Patrons were excited to be around when some of these things happened, but they were a little nervous too. So was Orsted. He'd been living at the inn since he bought it, but for two years in the mid-1990s he moved back to Estevan, commuting to work each day just so he could get a break from all the stress he felt at Kenosee Lake.

As word about the Moosehead's troubles spread, Canadian and American TV crews showed up to film the story of the haunted inn, and investigative reporters wrote about the creepy incidents experienced by Orsted, his girlfriend, his buddies and the servers working there. A psychic who read about the haunting phoned Orsted and told him his renovations to the place had probably upset the original owner, Archibald Grandison. She said that the old gentleman's spirit was most likely the source of the mournful moaning sound Orsted had started hearing outside his bedroom door.

Finally Orsted decided to take an "if you can't beat 'em, join 'em" approach to his weird predicament. He came up with the idea of hosting a psychic fair at the inn. Several people interested in ghosts and the paranormal showed up for the fair, which turned out to be quite an entertaining event for the whole town.

During the fair, Orsted took part in a special gathering, or seance, organized by a psychic who said she detected three separate ghosts at the inn. She claimed she was able to convince two of them — a cleaning woman and a teenaged boy who had drowned — to leave. But a third — an older man who may have been Archibald Grandison — seemed determined to stay around until he was certain his widow was being well cared for.

Mrs. Grandison was Orsted's next-door neighbour. He liked the elderly lady, and was already keeping a friendly eye on her, so he didn't mind at all making more of an effort to look after her. As soon as he started doing that, the number of spooky incidents decreased dramatically. In 1999, when Mrs. Grandison died, the ghost — and Orsted — finally found peace.

THE FiERY PHANTOM SHiP

Northumberland Strait,
Prince Edward Island

You've just spent a perfectly wonderful day on one of Prince Edward Island's sun-drenched beaches, just along the Northumberland Strait. You're packing up the picnic basket when you see it — a large ship, sails billowing. It appears out of nowhere and seems to be sailing danger- ously close to shore. You stare in amazement as you real- ize it's on fire. Then, as quickly as it appeared, it's gone.

If this happened to you, you would join the ranks of hundreds, maybe even thousands of others who have spotted a mysterious three-masted schooner sailing the waters off the southern shores of PEI. Your sighting would be a bit unusual because most appearances occur in the autumn, not in the summer, and often just before a stormy northeast wind blows in, not at the end of a warm, sunny day. But ever since the 1780s, the phantom ship has sailed into view in the spring, summer, winter and fall, in good and bad weather alike.

At times the schooner has even sailed right into Charlottetown Harbour, in clear view of scores of people working on the docks. Once, about a hundred years ago, several dockhands jumped into a dinghy and furiously rowed out to rescue the sailors they could see fighting the fires on deck. But just as they were about to reach the burning schooner, it was swallowed up in a murky mist. When the mist cleared just minutes later, no trace of the ship or its crew could be found.

It's easy enough to write off one person's story of the ship as the work of an overactive imagination, but reports from groups of witnesses such as those would-be rescuers in the harbour are much harder to ignore. Fifty years later a carload of teenagers spotted the ship in Victoria Harbour. They saw the crew moving around on deck and climbing up and down the rigging. They also saw the fires burning, but they watched long enough to note that the flames never consumed the ship. And in the early 1960s, people on a crowded beach were amazed when the burning schooner appeared late one afternoon.

No one story — a pirate's ship sunk off the coast, a vessel loaded with immigrants lost in a storm, a ship weighted down with lumber that disappeared without a trace — satisfies people's efforts to explain the presence of the ship in the area. But, together with the eerie sounds of cannon fire or "sea guns" that are often heard in the distance, the appearance of the phantom ship in the Northumberland Strait can still send shivers up the spines of many Islanders.

MURDERED FOR SILENCE

Hudson, Quebec

The Willow Place Inn can be found in Hudson, Quebec, a village 40 kilometres west of Montreal on picturesque Lac des Deux Montagnes. After a fire destroyed it in 1989, the inn was completely rebuilt and furnished in the style of the eighteenth-century building that had burned down.

The original structure was built in 1820 as a family home. In 1824, François Desjardins bought it and turned the main floor into a general store. But Desjardins was more than simple shopkeeper. He was also a member of the Patriotes, and, like the others in his group, he wanted to get rid of the appointed governing council that ignored the wishes of the elected assembly in favour of the rich and powerful. By the early 1830s, talk of rebellion was in the air. By 1837, Desjardins had started stockpiling guns and ammunition in his basement and was making his store available for secret meetings of the Patriotes who were fed up with government scandals and corruption.

At the time a young woman named Mary Kirkbride was working as a maid in the Desjardins' home. When she overheard some of the plans the Patriotes were making to organize an armed revolt, she felt she had to warn the authorities. Some say she ran away and reported what she'd heard. But others tell a more sinister story. They believe she was killed to keep her quiet, and her body was buried in the basement.

Over the years, the second version of events seemed to provide the best explanation for the spooky goings-on in the house. After Desjardins was sent to jail for taking part in the 1837 Rebellion of Lower Canada (Quebec), the Brasseur family bought his home and turned it into a boarding house. When they sold it, it became an inn, or *auberge*. In the 1970s people in Hudson started talking publicly about the ghostly activities that had been observed at the inn for some time.

Were the Willow's owners just spreading rumours to boost business? Not according to some of the staff. They, as well as the owners, saw furniture being pushed around by an invisible force. Often they were startled and nearly tripped when the basement door slammed shut behind them. Stones were heaped in front of a door to one of the guestrooms. And, from empty rooms and deserted hallways, they smelled perfume and heard the haunting sound of a woman singing.

Incidents like these don't seem to occur as often since the inn was rebuilt. But, as in the past, disturbing events usually happen between October 31 and the end of November. Skeptics aren't surprised that the apparent haunting begins on Halloween. What better night, they ask, for someone to claim to have seen, heard or even smelled a ghost? But the phantom is restless until the end of November. Fighting between Patriotes and government forces first broke out in the area in November 1837. Were plans for those skirmishes what Mary Kirkbride overheard and tried to report? If so, she would most likely have met her fate around the same time as many Patriotes met theirs — in the month of November.

Willow Place Inn

POSSESSION

Amherst, Nova Scotia

Sometimes a ghost haunts a person, not a place. Wherever that person goes, spooky things happen. Ghost experts usually blame this type of haunting on a particular kind of ghost — a poltergeist. Poltergeists are mischief-makers. They hide things, make scary noises and send stuff flying around a room. They don't hang around forever and they often pester a younger person. That description matches what happened to Esther Cox, but only up to a point. The poltergeist that targeted her didn't just pester her. For nearly a year, starting in September 1878, it made her life a living hell.

Cox was 18 when the nightmare began. At the time she was living in the home of her married sister, Olive, and Olive's husband, Daniel Teed. Her brother, William, and another sister, Jane, were also staying in the two-storey wooden house in Amherst. So were Daniel and Olive's young children and Daniel's brother, John. Esther and Jane shared a bedroom in the cozy, but crowded house.

One night in early September, Jane awakened to hear Esther whispering that there were mice in their bed. At first Jane thought her sister was just imagining things. Then she heard the scratching too. When both sisters jumped out of bed, they realized the sounds were coming from under the bed, not in it. They pulled out a low cardboard box of quilt patches, figuring the little rodents were building a nest in it. But as soon as they dragged the box into the middle of the room, it seemed to take on a life of its own. It shot up in the air, then tipped over on its side. A few seconds later, it took off and fell down again.

The sisters screamed for help. Their brother-in-law, Daniel, rushed in to see what was wrong. But when he heard what had happened, he said they must have been dreaming, and told them to go back to bed. The next night, though, all of the adults in the house came running into the bedroom when Jane screamed for help. What they found nearly turned their stomachs. As Esther screamed and writhed in pain on the bed, she began to swell up like a bloated corpse. Loud raps and snapping sounds filled the air, many of them coming from under the bed. Suddenly, after one ear-splitting bang, Esther's body deflated, and the wretched young woman fell into a deep sleep.

When a similar scene played out again four nights later, Esther's family asked the doctor to pay a visit. After listening to what he thought was a lot of nonsense, he told them that Esther was just suffering from a bad case of nerves. But right after he stated his diagnosis, Esther's pillow started moving back and forth and her blankets flew off the bed and across the room. The loud noises started again, but they weren't nearly as frightening as a new, softer, scratching sound that made everyone look above the bed. There, over the headboard, words began to emerge. The message, written by the unseen force, was chilling. "Esther Cox," it read, "you are mine to kill."

Fear filled the house from then on, and with good reason. The unnatural activities extended beyond Esther's bedroom. Something hammered on the roof and hurled potatoes around the basement. The knocking sounds took on a strange pattern and seemed to be an attempt at communication. It appeared that whatever was haunting the house was able to hear and see what was going on. When asked questions such as, "How many people are in the room now?" it answered with the correct number of knocks.

In December 1878, Esther became very ill. She spent two weeks in bed fighting diphtheria. Esther's family took very good care of her, but they couldn't help notice that her illness had brought them some blessed relief. Not once during those two weeks did anything unusual happen in the house. When Esther was well enough to travel, she went to stay for a few weeks with another married sister in Sackville, New Brunswick, giving the Amherst household another welcome break from the horror.

But shortly after Esther returned home in early January, things got worse. Along with the noises and moving objects, lit matches would appear out of thin air just below the ceiling and, still burning, drop to the floor. The danger of fire became very real — especially when Esther heard a voice telling her that the house was going to burn down. For the sake of her family, Esther had to go.

Esther's journey over the next several months was a lonely search for peace. Even going to church didn't bring her comfort. She had to stop attending regular Sunday services because the banging and hammering followed her there, disturbing others and leaving her humiliated. The Whites, a farming couple who needed extra help, took her in, but as much as they appreciated how hard she worked, they couldn't deal with the disappearing tools and flying objects.

In March 1879, Captain James Beck played host to Esther in Saint John, New Brunswick. Hoping to learn more about what was happening to her, he invited a group of people interested in after-death connections to meet with Esther and ask the haunting spirit some questions. They concluded that several ghosts were haunting Esther. Another man, Walter Hubbell, reached a similar conclusion.

Hubbell was an American actor who happened to be touring the Maritimes in 1879. Like so many others who had read the newspaper accounts of Esther's nightmare, Hubbell wanted to see for himself what was happening in Amherst. In June, not long after Esther had moved back home, Hubbell showed up at the family's house and was shocked by what he witnessed over the next several weeks. Later he would write a short book, *The Haunted House*, in which he told of a flying umbrella, a whizzing carving knife, chairs that broke on their own and, perhaps most disturbing of all, hundreds of pins that jabbed themselves into Esther's tormented body. Hubbell also reported spending time with Esther when, in a trance-like state, she talked about and even named the many invisible spirits that surrounded her.

At one point Hubbell tried to turn Esther's plight into

a moneymaking enterprise. He planned on touring with her, presenting her story as one would a play. But after just one appearance before a disappointed audience, he realized that Esther's ghosts wouldn't make themselves known on demand — something he had hoped would draw big crowds. Hubbell left town soon afterward, but his money-making efforts weren't entirely in vain. His book about what came to be known as "the great Amherst mystery" turned out to be a bestseller.

After Hubbell left, Esther managed to get a job working for an Amherst farmer named Arthur Davison. Like the Whites, the Davisons were willing to put up with a few flying objects and strange sounds — but not unexplained fires. When Davison's barn burned down, he blamed Esther. She was charged with arson, found guilty and sentenced to four months in jail. However, local townsfolk felt sorry for her and convinced authorities to release her after just one month.

Thankfully, by the end of 1879, the spirits that haunted Esther finally left her in peace. Eventually she married a man from Springdale, Nova Scotia, and had a little boy. When her first husband died, she remarried, moved to Massachusetts, and had another son. She died in November 1912, at the age of 52. Several years later, the cottage where the horror began for her was torn down to make way for new shops in downtown Amherst.

But Esther Cox's spirit lives on. The "great Amherst mystery" was written up in books and articles that were published around the world, and her nightmarish experience is still considered one of the most famous ghost stories on record.

MURDER REVEALED

Toronto, Ontario

Russian stonemason Ivan Reznikoff was pleased with his new job in Canada. Like several other foreign stonemasons, he had been encouraged to come to Toronto where his skills were in great demand. In 1858 he was working on the new University College building at the University of Toronto. The money was good, his savings were growing and he was in love. In fact, his girlfriend Susie had just accepted his marriage proposal.

One day, Reznikoff was carving the finishing touches on a large stone head, or gargoyle, that would peer down on passersby when it was done. Several other stonemasons worked alongside him on the detailed carvings that would decorate the upper levels of the building's exterior. During a break, one of the men leaned over and asked

Ivan if he recognized the gargoyle that another stonemason, a Greek named Paul Diabolos, was chiselling nearby.

At first glance Ivan didn't notice anything familiar about the head. The figures' mouths usually served as waterspouts draining rain off the roof, and their faces were usually distorted to look rather menacing. But when the man who had spoken to him pointed out that Diabolos was making the gargoyle look like Ivan, the young Russian saw what he meant. There was definitely a resemblance between himself and the Greek's wild-eyed stone creation. But why would Diabolos do this? Ivan wondered aloud. His co-worker replied the Greek was mocking him, because he hadn't realized that his fiancée, Susie, was seeing Diabolos despite her engagement to Reznikoff.

Though Reznikoff was filled with rage, he said nothing. Instead, he spent the rest of the day gouging out new features on his gargoyle to transform it into a hideous sculpture of Diabolos. And that night, armed with an axe, Ivan hid in the bushes near the arched walkway at the university where his informant had said the couple usually met. Right after dark he saw them — Susie and Diabolos — walking hand in hand along the path to the arch. He watched in silence as they sat on a bench and talked, heads close together as if sharing secrets. But when they embraced and kissed passionately, he lost control.

Reznikoff burst from the bushes and raced toward them, swinging the axe. Diabolos jumped up and ran for his life. He dashed into University College and closed the heavy oak door just in time to hear the axe hit it with a thud. He scrambled up a temporary set of wooden stairs in the unfinished stone tower and hid in an alcove. Reznikoff followed, but when he climbed out on the top platform, Diabolos lunged at him with a knife. After stabbing the Russian, he pushed Reznikoff over the edge of the platform and into the 25-metre-deep well where the tower's stone steps were to go.

Diabolos might have been able to make a good case for self-defence, but there's no record of that happening. There's also no evidence that anyone even bothered to report the unfortunate Reznikoff's sudden disappearance. But in the early 1860s, both professors and students started talking about a tall, handsome stranger they'd seen moving about the campus late at night. A few even said that he carried an axe. Whenever anyone tried to speak with him, he mysteriously disappeared.

One night a student named Allen Aylesworth was returning to his dormitory when he met a young man he didn't recognize. Assuming the fellow was a new arrival on campus, Aylesworth started up a friendly conversation with him. After a few minutes, he invited the stranger back to his room for a drink. After downing a couple of shots of whiskey, the stranger stunned Aylesworth by telling him something unbelievable. He said that his name was Ivan Reznikoff and that he was a ghost. He proceeded to talk about his beloved Susie, her betrayal of him with Diabolos and his horrible death at the hands of the Greek. Then he said goodnight and left.

When Aylesworth awoke the next morning, he remembered his encounter with Reznikoff, but he figured it must have been a bad dream. Ghosts — if they existed — didn't just come up and introduce themselves and join you for a drink. Then Aylesworth looked across the room. There on the table were two glasses and an empty liquor bottle.

Word of Aylesworth's eerie experience spread quickly around the university. From then on, whenever people spotted the ghostly apparition of a tall, heavy-set man

The quadrangle at University College, where the remains of Reznikoff are thought to be buried

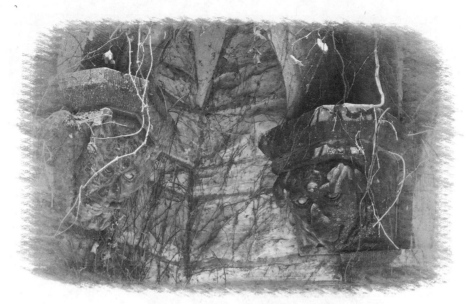

University College's gargoyles. Could these be the faces carved by Reznikoff and Diabolos?

around University College, they said it must be Reznikoff. In 1890 that explanation started sounding even more believable when the skeletal remains of a large unidentified male were dug up during construction near the base of the college tower. And when old records turned up showing that two stonemasons named Reznikoff and Diabolos had indeed worked at the college, more people became convinced that Aylesworth's tale must have been true. Anyone who still doubted Aylesworth's credibility as a witness, may have had second thoughts when he became a member of Parliament and was later knighted.

Then there's the gouge in the old oak door, said to be made by Reznikoff's axe. It's still there for all to see. And off to one side, glaring down from above, are two expertly carved stone gargoyles.

GHOST TRAIN

Buchans, Newfoundland and Labrador

In late 1927, the American Smelting and Refining Company finished work on a 35-kilometre railway line between Buchans and Millertown in Newfoundland's interior. The company built the line to ship the zinc, lead and copper ores dug out of the Lucky Strike mine in Buchans.

Soon after the line opened, the nearby Buchans River Dam burst, and surging water washed out the wooden train trestle across the river. Over the years, there were other accidents along the line, some of which claimed the lives of men who worked for the mining company. It's said that the spirits of those dead men might have been responsible for reported sightings of a ghost train in the area.

A few years after the Buchans line went into operation, people started talking about seeing a strange, distant light moving along the rails. Of course, it was much scarier for people who were on a train than for those who were standing off to the side of the tracks. That's because as the lights of the phantom train drew closer, it would appear as though another train was heading for a collision with the real one. At the very last second, just as the two trains seemed doomed to crash, the unidentified train would disappear.

Every now and then similar incidents were reported on other train lines in the province. There was also the occasional story about a ghostly conductor on a passenger train.

Today trains no longer operate in Newfoundland. The last one stopped running in 1989, and there haven't been any recent reports of ghost train sightings. But most of the tracks are still in place. What's to stop a phantom train from riding the rails through the Newfoundland backwoods even now? Might it happen again? Only time will tell . . .

THE WOMAN IN BLACK

Johnville, New Brunswick

On May 3, 2001, fire destroyed the Keenan covered bridge near Johnville, New Brunswick. Local residents were sad to lose such a vital part of the area's history. The wooden bridge had been built across the Monquart River in 1927 to replace the original covered span at that location. Many people were also saddened to think that something else had been lost to the flames — the ghost that had haunted both bridges for more than a hundred years.

Stories about the ghost began circulating in the late 1800s, when an older lady entered the bridge one day and was never seen again — at least, not alive. After her disappearance, people started talking about seeing a strange woman wearing old-fashioned black clothes on the bridge.

She never spoke to anyone, and she never stayed around when someone tried to approach her.

But the woman in black didn't seem to mind being the one to do the approaching. Silently, mysteriously and without any warning, she would suddenly appear in a wagon or sleigh — or in later years, even a car — sitting *beside* the person who was driving across the bridge. She would sit stiffly upright, staring forward with glazed, unseeing eyes. Worse still, sometimes she was headless.

To find oneself riding with such an apparition could be an absolutely terrifying experience. One farmer was crossing the bridge to visit his sister when he suddenly realized the woman in black was sitting right beside him on the wagon seat. He was frozen with fear. The reins hung limply in his hands, but his horse kept going. Then, as the wagon turned into his sister's lane on the other side of the bridge, he fainted.

When the man came to, the ghostly woman was gone and the horse was panicking. He pulled on the reins to stop the frightened beast, leaped off the wagon and rushed into his sister's house. But he was so stunned by what had happened that it took him a week to find the courage to talk about it.

Several people who encountered the woman in black were like that man. They didn't like talking about what they had seen. So, when Keenan Bridge was burned beyond repair, they must have been relieved. Surely, the ghost was gone forever. But imagine what they thought when they saw a photograph of the burned-out bridge that was taken by a transportation department worker. There, on a piece of smouldering timber, was the haunting image of a woman's face. Shortly after that picture was taken, the face on the charred timber disappeared.

A new bridge has been built across the Monquart River near Johnville. Only time will tell if the woman in black will visit it too.

The smouldering remains of Keenan Bridge.
Inset: Can you see a face?

THE TRAVELLING CORPSE

Fort McPherson, Northwest Territories

In 1852 Roderick Ross MacFarlane started working in the Northwest Territories as a clerk for the Hudson's Bay Company. He did his job well and quickly worked his way up through the ranks to become a factor, or manager. It was during MacFarlane's first few years with the company that he got to know Augustus Richard Peers. Peers was a successful fur trader who was put in charge of Fort McPherson, an isolated post north of the Arctic Circle.

When MacFarlane got the news that Peers had died in March 1853, he was sad to hear it. He had liked Peers. He also remembered hearing Peers say that he never wanted to be buried at Fort McPherson. But that was exactly what had happened to the trader's remains.

MacFarlane often thought about what the dead man

had said, but it would be nearly seven years before he got a chance to honour Peers' wishes. Late in 1859, he was at Fort McPherson on company business. Before leaving there for Fort Good Hope, where he was factor at the time, MacFarlane decided to take Peers' remains with him.

It wasn't easy digging the coffin out of the frozen ground, but the men assigned to the task finally managed to do it. However, when they hauled the coffin up, they saw that the years had taken their toll. Quickly they built a new, stronger casket. Then they opened the old one. Thanks to the chilly climate, Peers looked much the same as the day he had died. After getting over their shock at seeing how well-preserved the body was, the men carefully moved it to the new coffin, nailed the box shut and tied it to a sled.

After weeks of guiding dog teams and loaded sleds across rugged ice and through blinding snow, MacFarlane and his assistants finally reached Fort Good Hope early in 1860. But their journey wasn't over yet. All along, MacFarlane had planned to rebury Peers at Fort Simpson, which was still nearly 300 kilometres away. After he spent a few days accounting for furs they had picked up along the way, he got ready to hit the trail again. His men had nearly finished loading the sleds with supplies and trade goods for the next part of the journey when they realized there wasn't enough room for Peers' coffin. They removed his body from the box, wrapped it in a blanket and tied it to a sled. Then they were off again.

MacFarlane continued south along the Mackenzie River. The small group of travellers rested for a few days at Fort Norman (now Tulita) while MacFarlane conducted some more business. Then they continued moving south.

It was on March 15, 1860, the seventh anniversary of Peers' death, that the men started to feel very uncomfortable. They were setting up camp for the night close to the riverbank when the dogs started acting skittish. Then they began yelping and barking for no apparent reason. A little while later, the men started hearing voices, or more specifically, one voice. Time and again it called out from the darkness. "March," it said. "March."

MacFarlane and his crew searched the surrounding bush, but couldn't find the mysterious caller. They couldn't find what was continuing to upset the dogs, either. The animals kept barking and pawing the ground nervously, ignoring all efforts to calm them. Then, suddenly, they stopped shifting around, curled up and went to sleep. After calming their own nerves, the men finally fell asleep too.

The men heard the ghostly command to "march" once more before their journey ended. Later, MacFarlane would learn that Peers had used that word to urge on his dog team. Was the phantom voice that of Peers, urging the factor to keep moving until his remains were finally laid to rest? MacFarlane thought so, especially after Peers' ghost appeared to him when the group finally reached Fort Simpson. He was so terrified when he sensed the apparition's presence in his room that he hid under the covers in bed until it left.

MacFarlane arranged for Peers' remains to be buried in the Hudson's Bay Company cemetery at Fort Simpson. He stood by the grave as the body was lowered into the ground on March 23, 1860. But for years afterwards, he wondered if he had done the right thing. Were the ghostly cries a sign that Peers' spirit was eager to arrive at Fort Simpson? Or were they cries of complaint because his spirit was upset at having his grave disturbed in the first place? Whatever it was, MacFarlane was relieved when the ghost was still once more.

THE GHOST CHILD

Montreal, Quebec

Sir Arthur Conan Doyle, the creator of the fictional super-sleuth Sherlock Holmes, was very interested in ghosts and in communicating with the spirits of the dead. He often travelled to different cities in North America, giving lectures about the subject. In 1922, he visited Montreal as part of a Canadian lecture tour. There he read a newspaper article about a local couple coping with the presence of a poltergeist. Conan Doyle visited the couple, and what he learned about the haunting made such a strong impression on him that he wrote about it when he returned to England.

The middle-aged couple lived alone in their home, so when strange things started happening, they either had to blame each other or accept the fact that some unearthly force was at work. The man was slower to accept that fact than the woman was — not because he thought she was playing tricks on him, but because he didn't believe in ghosts.

So, when the lights went out time and again, suddenly plunging the house into darkness, he tried to convince her the wiring was faulty. When she was upset to find all the pictures in the house had been taken off the walls, he was curious, but not too worried about how that had happened. But when some invisible hand walloped him with a pillow on two separate occasions, his wife's belief that there was a ghost in their home no longer seemed so silly.

Conan Doyle recorded other eerie incidents that plagued the couple. The woman had kept a box of wooden blocks that their child had played with many years earlier. Several times, either when they got up in the morning or returned to the house together, the couple would be greeted with impressive block towers and buildings. Time after time, they would dismantle the structures and pack the blocks back in the closet, only to find them hauled out and stacked back up, as if a youngster had been having great fun playing with them.

Further evidence that the ghost might have been a child was babyish writing on bits of paper that mysteriously appeared in every room. However, other pieces of paper, covered with clearer lettering and detailed drawings, started showing up too, leading the owners and Conan Doyle to believe that two ghosts — a child and an adult — might be active in the house. Just thinking about such a possibility made the woman more nervous than ever.

The man arranged for a priest to visit and say prayers to drive out any unnatural forces that might be present in the house. But the haunting activity continued, and the couple finally decided they had no choice but to move. Fortunately for them, as Conan Doyle noted, the ghosts didn't move with them, and, after months of stress and fear, they finally found peace in a new home.

THE DOCTOR IS IN

Helmcken House, Victoria, British Columbia

Museums are like windows that offer views of times and places long past. Old houses that have been turned into museums are especially fascinating. As you move through their historically furnished rooms, you can imagine the people who lived there going about their daily tasks. Items such as dishes on the tables and handmade quilts on the beds give the impression that their original owners are expected back any minute.

Maybe imaginations work overtime in old places like these. Whatever the reason, it's not all that unusual for people touring them to report seeing and hearing some pretty spooky things. Helmcken House in downtown Victoria is an old house that has been turned into a museum.

It gives visitors a taste of what life in British Columbia was like about 150 years ago. Apparently some visitors have also experienced enough strange sights and sounds that the place is said to be haunted.

Helmcken House is the oldest house in British Columbia still in place on its original foundations. It started out as a three-room log home built by Dr. John Sebastian Helmcken in 1852. Dr. Helmcken had trained as a doctor in England, and came to Canada as a ship's surgeon for the Hudson's Bay Company. It was also as a doctor for the company that he settled at Fort Victoria. There, Helmcken fell in love and married Cecilia Douglas, the daughter of the colony's governor, Sir James Douglas. It was for Cecilia that the doctor built the first part of what was to become a large, stately home, and later, a museum.

Dr. Helmcken died in 1920, at the age of 96. His youngest daughter, Edith, who had gone to live with him after her husband died in 1896, continued to live in the house until her death in 1939. Soon after, the British Columbia government bought the house and, in 1941, opened it as a museum. Soon after that, the reports of unusual happenings began.

Every now and then someone sees a woman looking out a window on the second floor — even though there's no one in the house. Helmcken's wife, Cecilia, loved her new home, but she didn't get to live in it for very long. She died when she was just 31. It's said that she couldn't bear to leave the house forever, and that she's the woman in the window. There have also been reports of piano music coming from the house when it's empty.

Strange things happen when staff and visitors are in the house too. For example, lights go on by themselves, dishes are moved around the kitchen and thick, heavy doors swing open on their own.

Marc Vermette, a manager at the house, figures Dr. Helmcken and Edith are the invisible spirits who are making their presence known. Over the years he's come to think of them as friends. But a few unsuspecting workers and visitors have been very disturbed by their encounters with the ghosts of Helmcken House, and, for them, one visit to the museum has been one visit too many.

A person investigating the strange events at Helmcken House stands before the old piano that is said to play by itself. Some people have also pointed out the strange orb of light in this picture that mysteriously floats above the right side of the piano.

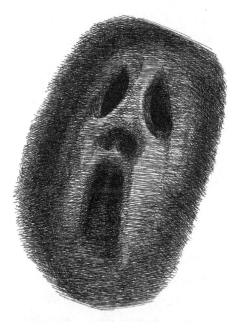

THE DUNGARVON WHOOPER

Miramichi, New Brunswick

If you ever heard the blood-curdling, ear-splitting cry of the Dungarvon Whooper, you wouldn't be easily convinced that the story behind the baleful moan was just a legend. Instead, you'd most likely join the ranks of those who've said over the years, "I heard it. It's true. There really is a ghost roaming the banks of the Dungarvon."

There are at least two versions of the story behind those horrible sounds, but the basic details are the same. Apparently sometime around 1860, a young man known only by his last name, Ryan, signed on to be the cook at a logging camp near the Dungarvon River, a branch of the Main Renous River in New Brunswick. Ryan was a friendly, outgoing fellow, well liked by the other loggers. He was also a bit too trusting for his own good. He made no secret of the fact that he kept his savings in a money belt he wore around his waist.

Every morning Ryan would make breakfast for the men. When it was ready, he would let out a loud, whooping yell to wake them up. Then he would pack their lunch pails and, after they left, set about baking and preparing supper.

One day, the foreman stayed behind with Ryan. What happened next depends on who's telling the story. One version has the boss murdering Ryan for his money, hiding his body under the snow and telling the other men that the cook had left while they were gone.

The more popular version has the foreman murdering Ryan for his money in the bunkhouse. When the other men returned to camp and found the young man's body on the floor, the boss told them Ryan had suddenly become ill and died. A fierce winter storm blew in that evening, piling up metre-high snowdrifts that stopped the crew from taking Ryan's body out of the bush for a proper funeral. The men were forced to bury his corpse in a shallow grave in the bush.

That night was a living hell for the men at the camp. The first nerve-wracking whoops pierced the silence of the forest shortly after dark. As the night went on, the horrifying wails grew louder, making sleep an impossibility. By morning the men had had enough. Convinced that they were hearing the mournful cries of the dead Ryan, they packed up and left the camp, vowing never to return.

Apparently, the foreman got away with murder, but it's as if Ryan's ghost found a way to make sure no one forgot his tragic end. For years afterwards, people reported hearing hair-raising screams if they found themselves near the place where Ryan was said to have been buried.

There were even reports of a ghost-like figure rising from the ground, screeching and wailing, if someone stepped too close to the supposed gravesite. Some sightings have the ghost swooping closer and closer until it hovers just overhead, filling the air with ear-splitting wails.

In the early 1900s a local priest, Father Edward Murdoch, travelled to the spot known as Whooper Spring and blessed the area to bring peace to Ryan's troubled soul — and to the people terrified by the unearthly sounds. Some say the prayers worked, and that the woods around the gravesite were quiet at last. Others say that wasn't the case, and that reports of the haunting screams still continue to filter out of the forest.

The Dunvargon Whooper is probably New Brunswick's most famous ghost. In 1912 Michael Whelan, known as the Poet of Renous, published a ballad called *The Dungarvon Whooper*. In it he recounted all the details about the ghost that he'd heard over his lifetime. And a train that ran through the region until 1936 also kept the story of Ryan's murder in people's minds. Perhaps it was because the train was often loaded with rowdy lumberjacks, whooping it up as they went to and from the bush. Or maybe it was because of the haunting sound the whistle made as the train rumbled by. Whatever the reason, the train was known as the Dungarvon Whooper.

RESCUE FROM THE GRAVE

Fox River, Nova Scotia

As a sea captain, George Hatfield was often away from his home at Fox River, west of Parrsboro, for months at a time. In March 1876, he was still a few weeks from home, sailing north from Cuba to Boston in stormy Atlantic waters. After a harrowing day at the helm, Hatfield decided to go below for some much-needed sleep. Soon after he nodded off, he felt a hand on his shoulder and heard someone tell him to alter his course. But when he rolled over and looked around his cabin, there was nobody there.

Hatfield figured his first mate must have left right after delivering his message, so he headed back up to the bridge to find out what was going on. When he got on deck, he found his mate at the wheel, carefully steering the ship through the treacherous waves. Hatfield asked the man why he didn't want to follow the course that had been set, but the mate had no idea what his captain was talking about.

Hatfield felt more than a little foolish. Deciding that he must have dreamed the visitor to his cabin, he went below and stretched out on his bunk again. But once more his sleep was interrupted in exactly the same way. Angry, he went back up to ask the first mate why he wanted to change course and why he hadn't stayed to discuss the matter after waking him up. The poor mate said he hadn't left his post, nor had any other member of the crew.

Confused, Hatfield tried once more to get some rest. He had barely closed his eyes when he again felt someone tapping his shoulder and ordering him in a firm, loud voice to make a specific course change. This time, though, when the captain looked up, he saw a man he didn't recognize leaving his cabin. He jumped up and hurried back up the stairs. When he reached the first mate, he asked him if he had just seen someone walking along the deck. The mate said no. Hatfield looked around for a few seconds, then turned to the worried man and ordered him to alter the ship's course in the way the voice had described. Then the captain returned to his cabin and fell into a deep sleep.

The mate was afraid his captain might be suffering from extreme exhaustion, but he did as he was told. He was still steering the new course when Hatfield appeared back on deck the next morning, looking rested but anxious. Hatfield ordered his crew to keep a close watch on the sea ahead. A few hours later he heard a cry that he seemed to be expecting. One of his men had spotted a battered ship that appeared to be taking on water at a deadly rate.

Through a series of dangerous manoeuvres, Hatfield

and his crew managed to get close enough to the American schooner *D. Talbot* to rescue everyone on board. The schooner's captain, a man named Amesbury, was especially grateful to Hatfield. His wife and child were among those rescued.

After Amesbury and his family had dried off and had a warm drink, Hatfield sat down with them and told them how he had found them. As he was describing the strange man who had mysteriously appeared in his cabin, Mrs. Amesbury interrupted him and asked for more details about what the man looked like and what he was wearing. Then she started to cry. When Hatfield asked her what was wrong, she told him he had just described her father. In a trembling voice she went on to explain that her father had died ten years earlier.

Is it possible that Mrs. Amesbury's father cared for her so much that he'd returned from the grave to save her from certain death? Who else could have appeared to Hatfield in the middle of the Atlantic and guided him to the exact spot, in that vast ocean, where his help was needed the most?

THE PROSPECTOR'S SPECTRE

O'Brien Creek, Yukon Territory

Fred Nelson looked as if he had seen a ghost. That's because he had — just a few days earlier. Even back in the safety of Dawson, he was still filled with fear as he spoke of what had happened at the mouth of O'Brien Creek, near what came to be known as Fortymile.

A reporter with the Klondike Nugget carefully observed Nelson as he told his horrifying tale. He noted how Nelson's eyes had a wild look about them, and his hands trembled. His voice even cracked as he gave a detailed account of what he and another gold prospector, a man called Swanson, had seen and heard in a two-room cabin in the wilderness. By the time Nelson had finished his story, the reporter was convinced that it was true. No man could pretend to be that scared.

Like most people in the area back then, Nelson and Swanson had heard rumours that the cabin was haunted. It had sat abandoned for 14 years, ever since its owner, a prospector named La Salle, had been found dead there in 1886. From the bloodied state of La Salle's body, it was clear that he had been murdered. Suspicion had fallen on some Tanana men from Alaska who were fed up with the fur traders, miners and missionaries that kept invading their territory. However, there was no proof that they had killed La Salle, and no one was ever charged with the crime.

For years after La Salle's death, stories circulated about strange sounds coming from the cabin. Those few daring enough to go near it — Indigenous and non-Indigenous people alike — told of being overcome by a creepy feeling as they approached the door. That weird feeling was enough to send them on their way without going inside.

But the temperature had plunged to nearly 40 degrees below zero on the evening that Nelson and Swanson spotted the cabin in the distance. Faced with the very real possibility of freezing to death, they decided to take shelter in it and hope for the best. They were nervous when they went inside, but once they got a small fire going in the old stove, they felt much calmer. Eventually they fell asleep.

At first Nelson thought it was the howl of the wind that woke him up around midnight. But as he rolled over to get comfortable, he heard the sound again. It wasn't the wind and it wasn't coming from outside. It was the sound of someone moaning and it was coming from the back room. Swanson was awake by then. He had heard the moans too.

Nelson jumped up and pushed on the door connecting

the two rooms, but even though it had swung open freely earlier, it was now stuck. Swanson rammed it with his shoulder, but it wouldn't budge. At that point Nelson thought he heard a low voice weakly pleading for help. As he pulled on his parka, he shouted at Swanson to keep trying to open the door. Then he jammed his feet into his boots and headed outside.

Nelson ran around the side of the cabin, intending to break the small window in the back room. But when he got to it, it was filled with an eerie light. Looking inside he saw the misty apparition of a man with a horrible gash on the side of his head. Petrified, Nelson stumbled back into the cabin and, nearly choking with fear, told Swanson what he had seen.

Swanson backed away from the door, no longer wanting to open it. But the moans grew louder, so he edged nearer and, in a loud voice, told whatever was in the room to identify itself. Over the next several minutes, he asked questions and got patterns of knocks in reply. When Swanson asked if the phantom was La Salle's ghost, the knocks got louder, and when he asked the spirit who had killed him, the door suddenly burst open. Filling the doorway was the glowing image of a man, his arms stretched upwards. Both Swanson and Nelson screamed, but before they could make it outside, the figure vanished.

Both prospectors managed to find the courage to stay in the cabin long enough to pack up their gear. Then they slipped out into the darkness, preferring to take their chances with the deadly cold rather than spend another minute in the shelter of La Salle's cabin.

PHANTOM OF THE EMPRESS

Fort Macleod, Alberta

Fort Macleod is the oldest town in Alberta. About 160 kilometres south of Calgary, it's where the North West Mounted Police (now the Royal Canadian Mounted Police) built their first post in the province in 1874. A reconstruction of the original fort is the town's main tourist attraction.

Fort Macleod is also home to the Empress Theatre, the province's longest operating live theatre. Since opening in 1912, the theatre has always been one of the town's main gathering places. Variety shows, concerts, musicals, plays and lectures — the Empress has hosted them all. It's also been *the* place to go to take in the latest hit movie.

But every now and then the Empress Theatre plays host to an eerie performance that isn't on the list of scheduled events. It's a one-person show, starring a character that theatre staff call Ed. Who Ed is remains a mystery, and what he does is very mysterious too. Those who've seen him say he's a big, hairy fellow who holds his trousers up with suspenders. One show manager reported seeing him in the audience, sitting in the same place in the balcony several nights running. An actor said that Ed actually stood on the stage for a while during an evening performance. And once a customer said he bought tickets from an older, rather large man he didn't recognize, only to learn later that no men were working in the box office that particular night.

Some people say that Ed must be the ghost of a janitor who worked at the theatre more than 70 years ago. No one knows how that man died, but apparently he smoked and drank a lot. He also worked part-time at a local cattle auction. That could explain why smells of tobacco, alcohol and manure linger in the air whenever the ghost makes an appearance. When it once looked as though the Empress would have to close, the sound of crying could be heard in empty dressing rooms. Perhaps the Empress's most faithful janitor couldn't bear to have the theatre close.

Of course, if Ed is the spirit of a long-dead janitor, he seems to have forgotten how hard it is to take care of a theatre. Supposedly he's the culprit who occasionally tosses trash out onto the floor, right after it's been put in the garbage can. He is also blamed for hiding things, setting off the security alarms, slamming doors and flipping the seats up and down. People have also reported hearing someone running in the aisles, even though they can't see anyone there.

Theatre managers say that Ed is a harmless ghost whose antics can be annoying at times. But wouldn't you feel more scared than annoyed if you saw coffee mugs moving around on a table when no one was touching them? And what would you think if you saw footprints forming in a sawdust-covered floor, as if some invisible person were walking across the room? Ed is said to have been responsible for both of those spooky performances.

One theatre patron also said that the image of a stranger suddenly appeared behind him in the mirror — when he was alone in the washroom. When he described the apparition to the staff, they agreed that it sounded just like Ed. But that's the only time he's been seen in the washroom, so theatregoers shouldn't be afraid to use the facilities at the Empress. Still, no one can be sure where or when Ed might show up next. Unlike other performers at the theatre, Ed doesn't advertise his appearances ahead of time.

WAILS OF SORROW

Signal Hill,
Newfoundland and Labrador

Signal Hill in St. John's is one of Newfoundland and Labrador's best-known landmarks. Hike to the top of it and you'll be rewarded with spectacular views of the city and harbour below, the rugged coastline on either side of the narrow harbour entrance and the seemingly endless stretch of ocean beyond it. You'll also have a chance to tour Cabot Tower, the tall castle-like museum on top of the hill. It was built in 1897 to celebrate the 400th anniversary of John Cabot's arrival in the New World.

Signal Hill is also the place where, on December 12, 1901, inventor Guglielmo Marconi received the first trans-Atlantic wireless radio signal. But that's not why the steep rocky rise is called Signal Hill. From the early

1700s, flags that identified approaching ships were flown from a post on the hill to signal to the traders and dock-workers below which ships would soon be sailing into the harbour.

Over the centuries Signal Hill has also played an important role in Newfoundland's defence. It was the ideal place to position batteries — groups of cannon — that could be aimed at any invading ships that tried to enter the harbour. At different times barracks were also built on the hill to house garrisons of soldiers and their families. Scaffolds were erected on the hill too. The shocking sight of hanged criminals dangling high above the port served as a powerful reminder of the price to be paid for crimes such as treason and murder.

With such a colourful history, it shouldn't come as a surprise to learn that a ghost is said to haunt Signal Hill. What may be surprising is that the ghost is believed to be female. Many times people have reported hearing the mournful wail of a woman. The sadness in her cry is unmistakable. But who might she be?

One possible explanation is that she was the wife of a young soldier stationed at one of the barracks on the hill in the early 1840s. Those barracks were terrible places to live in the winter. Constantly battered by icy winds, they were almost impossible to keep warm. In an 1842 report Governor John Harvey referred to "the extreme sufferings" endured by the barracks' soldiers and their families. He described how the chimneys couldn't draw smoke up out of the fireplaces, leaving people with two choices — put out the fires or open the windows to vent the smoke-filled rooms. Either way, the barracks were left bone-chillingly cold.

Things got so bad that more than a dozen frostbitten

Cabot Tower on Signal Hill

Royal Artillery soldiers had to be hospitalized. Worse still, a young mother who had tried to sit up all night holding her baby to keep it warm, woke up the next morning to find it dead in her arms. Harvey was horrified when he found out about the infant's tragic death. He ordered the barracks closed immediately and moved the company down the hill to warmer quarters.

Some say it's the dead baby's mother whose wails have been heard on Signal Hill. But perhaps the heartbroken spirits of other women have also lingered high above the harbour. Many wives and girlfriends used to climb the hill each morning to gaze out at the steely grey Atlantic, hoping for a glimpse of an overdue ship or boat. Often those women waited in vain. Their wails — the cries of women from long ago, whose men were lost at sea — may still blow across the rocky crest of Signal Hill.

SOLDIER FOR ALL ETERNITY

Niagara-on-the-Lake, Ontario

"Swayze's Cellar" — the sign on the wooden plank door says it all. The cellar of the Olde Angel Inn in Niagara-on-the-Lake is Captain Colin Swayze's hangout. The inn's owners don't know when he returned to the basement, but they accept the fact that he has. They even humour him by flying a British Union Jack flag outside. Of course the cellar isn't the most comfortable spot to hang out. Guests have commented how cold it can get down there. But the captain doesn't seem to mind the unusually chilly drafts. He may even be causing them. After all, Swayze has been dead for nearly 200 years.

A British soldier, Swayze fought in Canada against the Americans during the War of 1812. When American invaders showed up at the inn in 1813, Swayze hid in a rum barrel in the cellar. One version of his death has him being killed during a hand-to-hand fight when the enemy found him. Another version has the Americans stabbing him with their bayonets as he crouched in the barrel.

Not long afterward, American forces burned down the inn, and it wasn't rebuilt and expanded until the 1820s. Back then it offered travellers good food, cozy rooms and friendly service. It still does, but over the years it has also offered former and current owners and guests some very strange experiences.

Several years ago a man in a red coat made some sudden appearances — and disappearances — in the women's washroom in front of two startled cleaning ladies. They seem to be the only ones who've actually seen the ghostly figure of an army officer from the past.

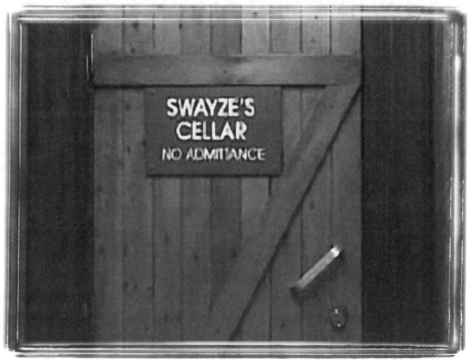

The door to Swayze's Cellar

But Florence LeDoux, a former owner who also lived at the inn as a child, once saw three saucers float through the air, one behind the other, before crashing to the floor several metres away. Her head waiter, Bruce Cartwright, was nearly hit in the head when a metal beer mug was whipped across the lounge by some invisible hand.

And then there are the footsteps — eerie and plodding — when no one else is around. People have been hearing the footsteps late at night for as long as anyone can remember. There have also been reports of dishes rattling in a cupboard, chairs moving across the floor and the sound of a man's laughter coming from the empty dining room.

Occasionally a guest has heard fife-and-drum marching music coming from a second floor bedroom. No one's been able to discover who — or what — is playing it, but it is the sort of music Captain Swayze and his men would have bravely marched to nearly 200 years ago.

Swayze's death may have stopped him from fighting in the war, but it seems that he will never surrender to death.

THE DEAD LIGHTS

St. Louis, Saskatchewan

St. Louis, Saskatchewan is a small town with a big story to tell. Located about 40 kilometres south of Prince Albert, it's the place to go if you want to hear about — and maybe even see — the St. Louis light.

The ghostly light has been appearing just north of St. Louis for more than 80 years. It shows up often enough that some locals take houseguests out for a midnight drive just to get a glimpse of it. The light rarely lets them down. Young people go out to wait for it too, just for the fun of it. Sometimes, though, seeing it can be more frightening than funny.

Saskatoon residents Serge and Gail Gareau thought it would be entertaining to take friends visiting from Alberta to see the famous light. They arrived in St. Louis about an hour before midnight, and parked outside the town beside the old railway tracks that hadn't been used for years. There was a chill in the air, so they stayed in the car, chatting and waiting. After about an hour, they were ready to head back to Saskatoon. Then it happened. First the light appeared as a small white circle, but then it grew a little larger and brighter and it seemed to get closer and closer. Beneath the white light was a smaller red one.

Amazed, the four friends stayed in the car and watched the lights for more than an hour. It still seemed as though the beams were getting closer, but they never actually did, so Serge and his buddy decided to go toward them and check them out. They started the car and edged out onto a bumpy dirt road that ran beside the old rail line. After they'd been driving for a few minutes, the lights suddenly went out.

But, just a few seconds later, an eerie glow filled the car. All four turned around, and, to their horror, saw that the light was now behind them — and it was much too close for comfort. Amid shrieks and shouts to get out of there, Gareau sped back toward the main road at top speed. As they drove away, they could see that the light was gone again.

Documentary filmmakers, a university professor and even a mayor of St. Louis, Emile Lussier, have all gone on record as having seen the light. Distant headlights have been offered as one explanation for its fairly regular appearance, but Lussier said experts investigated and rejected that possibility. Besides, people were seeing the light as far back as the 1920s, when hardly anyone in the area owned a car.

But trains were still running past St. Louis then, and some locals recall a story about a tragic accident on the tracks near their town. Details are vague, but the story has a worker carrying a lantern as he walked along the tracks checking for loose rails. The unfortunate man was struck by a locomotive, and the blow was so powerful that it ripped off his head.

The train tracks were pulled up years ago, but some people believe that horrifying death scene is still being played out every time the light appears. The white light is the headlight of the engine that hit the man, and the smaller red light is the lantern he was holding when it sent him to his death.

THE VANISHING VISITOR

Summerland, British Columbia

Summerland nestles on the western shore of Okanagan Lake, a few minutes drive north of Penticton. Home now to more than 10,000 residents, it was a small farming community when World War I was raging in Europe. Back then newcomers to the area — many from Manitoba — were still planting thousands of fruit trees in what would soon become Canada's world-famous Okanagan Valley orchards.

One family (whose members wanted to remain anonymous) settled on the outskirts of Summerland and welcomed the valley's peace and quiet even more so as bloody battles were being fiercely fought abroad. The parents were grateful to still have their two boys at home, both because they were safe and because they could help out with all the work that had to be done in the apple orchard.

But one night, as the two young men finished up the day's chores, they felt anything but safe. They had gone out to move their horse to a grassier part of the meadow beside the orchard. While they were re-tying it, a sudden movement in the distance caught the younger brother's eye. Across the pasture, he saw a man walking along the lonely road that ended just past their orchard. Since their family's farm was the last one on the road, the boy couldn't help but wonder where the man had come from. He also wondered who he was.

It was hard to see the man's face clearly in the moonlight, but both brothers felt sure he was a stranger to the area. He was solidly built, and, as he got closer, they saw that he was wearing a white hip-length jacket buttoned high at the neck. It looked a lot like an old-fashioned type of lounge jacket that a country gentleman might have worn years before. The younger brother called out a greeting, and asked where he was going. The man turned, looked right at him, then turned away without saying a word and kept right on walking toward the farmhouse. The boys lost sight of him as he strolled past the front of their house to the side door.

The brothers headed home quickly. They were eager to meet the mysterious night visitor. But when they opened the door into the kitchen, they saw only their parents, sitting at the table. When they asked where the stranger was, their parents looked puzzled. They said no one had come to the door and they had heard no one knocking or walking around outside.

"But that can't be. He was just here," the brothers said, and they explained to their parents what they had seen and heard. Or, more significantly, what they had not heard. It suddenly dawned on the younger brother that the man had not only remained silent when spoken to, but had also not made a sound when he walked. Neither brother had heard a single footstep as the stranger strolled confidently along the road past them on that still, moonlit night.

That the man hadn't spoken wasn't too unusual: he could have simply been rude or unwilling to talk. But no person could walk along a road like that without making a sound. So who, or what, was the man?

In the next few weeks, the brothers casually asked neighbours if they had seen any strangers in the area recently. No one had. The young men never let on why they were asking, because they didn't want folks to guess what they suspected must have happened that evening. Even 40 years later they wouldn't use their real names when they spoke about how the two of them, together, on a quiet, moonlit night, had seen and tried to speak to a ghost.

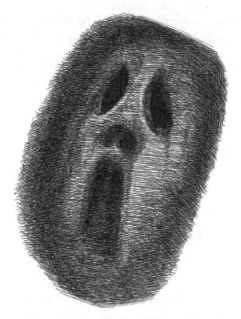

HEADLESS HARVIE

Windsor, Nova Scotia

In the winter of 1906 George Stanley chopped off Freeman Harvie's head and hid the gory remains in his basement. Then Stanley claimed Harvie had left town and given him all his worldly goods, but some folks in Windsor became suspicious. A search of Stanley's place soon turned up the decapitated body. Stanley was charged, tried and convicted of murder, and in the summer of 1906 he was hanged for his crime.

Not long afterward, Judge Charles Edgar DeWolfe reported seeing an apparition of a headless man in a basement window. Knowing that parts of Harvie's corpse had been found hidden under a pile of potatoes in a basement, DeWolfe was certain that what he had seen was the ghost of the unfortunate murder victim. Others who heard his story weren't so sure. But a few days later, DeWolfe became even more convinced that's what had happened.

The judge was walking home, his mind on other things, when an empty barrel appeared out of nowhere. It rolled along Water Street, crossed the road, changed directions, kept on rolling along the sidewalk and then turned sharply on to his front lawn. The judge couldn't believe his eyes. It was as if some invisible hand had been pushing the barrel all the way there. When he caught up to the barrel, he couldn't believe his ears either. Low, mournful groans were coming from the barrel. Then a voice spoke. "I am Freeman Harvie," it moaned. Terrified, Judge DeWolfe steered clear of the barrel and scurried into his house.

From then on, almost every time he went out, the judge came across more evidence of a ghostly visitor. As he passed a few boys on the sidewalk, they suddenly went into zombie-like trances, as did a couple of clerks when he went into stores to shop. The boys and the clerks would stay frozen, eyes staring straight ahead, until the judge — who had done a lot of reading about hypnotism — spoke to them in a soothing voice and waved his hands slowly past their faces. Only then would they snap out of their trances. Before DeWolfe's eyes, old coins would fall from the sky and light bulbs would smash to the ground in front of him. Chairs started rocking on their own when he dropped into the town's furniture factory, and strange voices called out his name. It was as if a mischievous ghost had possessed the entire town.

Judge DeWolfe became more and more concerned about what was happening. In an attempt to find an explanation for the mysterious events, he wrote to an organization that took a scientific approach to investigating claims of ghostly hauntings. He even sent along signed statements from other people in Windsor who claimed that unexplained events had been happening to them as well. That group sent Hereward Carrington, a young reporter and magician, to check out DeWolfe's story.

After DeWolfe gave Carrington a detailed account, they toured some of the places in Windsor where the eerie incidents had occurred. At the grocery store, an apple flew across the room, barely missing Carrington's head. Carrington was amazed, but still not convinced some unearthly force had moved it. He couldn't help noticing that even though the grocer's hands were on the counter, the shopkeeper blushed when the apple took off. At the furniture factory, Carrington listened carefully as sincere-sounding workers explained how they'd been just as frightened as the judge when chairs spontaneously fell over and the pipes started making weird knocking noises. Suddenly Carrington himself was startled by some rocking chairs that began to move back and forth on their own.

Excited by the possibility of finally finding real evidence of a poltergeist's presence, Carrington still took time to examine the rocking chairs very carefully. That's when he found the first signs of human, not ghostly, hands. Behind the chairs he found a hole in the floor. Coming out of the hole was a string that had been looped through each of the chairs. One pull from the basement below could start all the rockers moving.

But Carrington said nothing about what he had found and continued touring the factory. Pipes started banging, furniture fell over and coins dropped to the floor. One man even went into a trance, but Carrington noted that the supposedly frozen fellow had trouble stifling a laugh. The reporter was now certain that he was observing pranksters at their best, but he still said nothing to the unfortunate judge.

However, when the two men moved on to other shops in town, various culprits decided to tell the truth. One young woman admitted to throwing some paper to the floor in the stationery store, and two young men confessed they had just been pretending when the judge had found them acting like zombies. But Judge DeWolfe wouldn't believe them.

When Carrington decided to go out again without the judge, more people came forward to tell him that they had also been in on the joke. For that's what it had been — a practical joke played at the expense of Judge DeWolfe. It had all started innocently enough when two boys who were playing with the barrel let it get away from them. When they saw how alarmed the judge was by the runaway barrel, they decided to play a trick on him. They, like the rest of the town, knew that the judge had claimed to see the headless ghost. Before he got to his front gate, one of them hid in the barrel, moaned and groaned and said he was Freeman Harvie.

When DeWolfe reported Harvie's second appearance, the boys bragged about what they had done. After that, more people came up with other mischief-making schemes, assuming the judge would quickly figure out what was going on. But he didn't. Even when he read Carrington's final report on the nature of the "haunting" weeks later, he clung to his interpretation of what had happened. Perhaps he had trouble accepting the facts because his feelings would have been so hurt if they were true. But maybe there was another reason for his reluctance. After all, he had seen the headless ghost in the window, and Carrington was never able to disprove that eerie appearance.

A PARANORMAL PRESENCE

Gagetown, New Brunswick

In 1941 M. Patricia Jenkins, one of Canada's best-known weavers, bought a large two-storey house in Gagetown, New Brunswick. Called Roseneath, the house had been built in 1810 by Hugh Johnston Jr., a rich local business-man and politician.

Jenkins loved her home, and liked having houseguests. But some of her visitors weren't as comfortable at Roseneath as she was. Several of them felt that there was an invisible presence in the house. One old friend who came for the weekend stayed up all night reading so she wouldn't fall asleep. She not only felt the presence, but also sensed that it wasn't thrilled with her being there. Another visitor told Jenkins she felt the presence as soon as she walked through the door, and she got the impression that a sad-looking, red-cheeked man was standing on the stairs when she arrived.

Jenkins herself had noticed something a little unusual about her house shortly after she moved in. She had decided to replace the dark, rusty-brown wallpaper in the living and dining rooms. After scraping off several layers of old paper, she was amazed to find that the original layer was almost identical to the paper she had bought. At the time she had just thought it was a wonderful coincidence. After some of her friends started talking about the strange feeling they got in her house, she wasn't so sure.

Jenkins started asking questions about Roseneath. The people she had bought the place from told her they had often heard strange noises for which they could find no cause. What's more, a clergyman friend had seen the ghostly apparition of a woman several times when he visited them. Stephen Hall, an elderly gentleman whose parents owned the house in the early 1900s, remembered hearing creepy noises coming from different parts of the house too. He also told Jenkins that there had been stories about eerie lights that moved along the hall and up the stairs to the attic.

Jenkins started seeing Roseneath in a new light. Although she hardly ever sensed a strange presence herself, she accepted the fact that others felt a ghostly spirit also called Roseneath home. But that possibility didn't frighten her; in fact, it was even a little comforting. At least it gave her an explanation for some of the other weird things that happened at the house over the years. For instance, she could blame the ghost's taste in art for the trouble she had trying to hang a new painting.

A group of friends had pitched in to buy the picture for Jenkins, and she wanted to hang it in a place where they could see how much she loved their gift. She chose what she thought was the perfect place for the large forest scene — above the fireplace in the living room. The next morning she found the painting propped up on the mantel. The hook was still securely nailed to the wall and the wire loop attached to the picture frame was still intact, so it was clear that the painting hadn't just fallen down onto the mantel.

Three more times Jenkins tried to hang the painting — on another wall in the living room, above the fireplace in her bedroom and over a low bookcase in the hall upstairs. Each time the painting would be taken down, but not by Jenkins or anyone else visiting her. Finally, Jenkins tried hanging the painting in the living room again, on a wall opposite the windows that looked out on the yard. The next morning, the picture was still in place. It was never moved again.

Did the mysterious presence in the house want the picture hung where she couldn't see it? Or did she want it hung where she could look in at it if she were outside in the garden? There was a spot in the yard where, despite every gardening effort, absolutely nothing ever grew. Jenkins used to joke that the bare spot might be where her invisible housemate did her exercises. But perhaps the resident spirit did spend time outside and liked to see the painting from her favourite spot in the garden.

Jenkins didn't worry too much about why the painting was moved. She wasn't even seriously worried about whether or not her house was haunted. After all, she never actually saw any ghostly figure roaming around Roseneath. She admitted that she often turned around because she felt someone had just come into the room, only to find no one there. But she figured that sort of thing happened to everybody, no matter where they lived.

But did everybody else's cat act the way hers did when that sort of thing happened? Did their pets suddenly look up, eyes large with fear, and slowly turn their heads as if they were watching someone move around the room? Did they act as if they had just seen a ghost? Jenkins' cat did, and she couldn't help but wonder why.

A GHOST NIGHT'S SLEEP

Winnipeg, Manitoba

Like most grand old hotels, the Fort Garry Hotel in Winnipeg has strong links with the past. It was built in 1913, close to where Upper Fort Garry once stood. The fort was built way back in 1835, on the site of an earlier trading post. In 1870 the famed Métis leader, Louis Riel, captured it during the Red River Rebellion.

But a connection to history isn't the only thing many grand old hotels have in common. Like several others, the Fort Garry Hotel is said to be haunted.

For years, guests at the Fort Garry have reported feeling as if they weren't alone when they stayed in certain rooms. But those reports haven't stopped hundreds of guests from returning to the hotel year after year. In fact, a few specifically ask for a room that is rumoured to be haunted.

But what if, one night, the rumour became a reality? Suppose you fell asleep in such a room, and woke up a few hours later because you felt the mattress move, as if someone — or something — had lain down beside you? Would you just tell yourself you were dreaming and fall back asleep?

That's what Brenda Chamberlain, a member of parliament from Ontario, did when that happened to her at the Fort Garry. About 30 minutes later, Chamberlain woke up again. This time she had felt the invisible presence shift its weight on the mattress, as if it were trying to get more comfortable. At that point, a more timid person might have grabbed a robe and headed down to the main desk to demand a new room. But Chamberlain didn't. Somehow she managed to stay calm, and even got a few more hours of sleep.

Chamberlain was lucky, though. She probably wouldn't have stayed so calm if she had seen what some house-cleaning staff say they've seen in one second floor room — streaks of blood running down the walls. And she might have been at least a little upset if a woman in a long white dress had floated at the end of her bed before drifting out the window. That's what one guest said she saw when she stayed at the hotel.

A story about a doomed couple in love may explain the presence of haunting spirits at the Fort Garry. It's said that a young woman ran away years ago to stay with her boyfriend at the hotel. Her father and brothers supposedly found the couple there and murdered the boyfriend. Crazed with grief, the young woman hanged herself in the closet. Another similar story has a young woman hanging herself in the closet after finding out that her husband had just been killed in a car accident.

Whatever the reason for her suicide, the grief-stricken young woman is said to wander the hotel in search of her lover. Some people believe that she died in the room where the blood appears on the walls and that she's the woman in the white gown. Could she or her boyfriend also be the ghostly visitor who slips into guests' beds? Some people say yes, and that the two lovers are trying to find each other and be together again.

But the story of the dead couple doesn't seem to explain what happened at the hotel back in 1989. Two staff members were cleaning up the kitchen after 3 a.m. when they heard a noise in the dining room. The room was locked up for the night, and there wasn't supposed to be anyone in there. Quietly, the two men pushed open the swinging door from the kitchen. What they saw surprised them. Sitting at a table was a man who seemed to be thoroughly enjoying eating the dinner set out in front of him. They had never seen him before, and they hadn't served him any food.

The workers slipped out to the front desk to ask the night manager if he knew who the man in the dining room was. He had no idea what they were talking about. Curious, he went back to the kitchen with them and pushed open the swinging door. The dining room was dark and silent, and there was no sign of the man or the food he'd been eating.

Was that middle-of-the-night diner another ghostly visitor checking into the Fort Garry Hotel? Perhaps. Who else could he have been?

The Fort Garry Hotel

FRiGHTENED TO DEATH

Scotchfort, Prince Edward Island

People keep on talking about some strange and scary events long after they happen. What happened to Peter MacIntrye was so terrifying that some people still talk about it more than 200 years later.

MacIntyre was one of the hundreds of Highlanders who sailed from Scotland in the late 1700s in search of a better life. Like many others, his destination was Prince Edward Island, known back then as St. John's Island. The last stop on his voyage was a place named Scotchfort, about 30 kilometres north of Charlottetown.

For MacIntyre and the other new arrivals, life was hard but it was good. They quickly settled in, clearing land, building houses and planting crops. Before long, they began to feel right at home.

One evening, MacIntyre decided to head over to the general supply store where local men often gathered for a chat. Just as he had hoped, he found a few of his neighbours sitting around the wood stove, talking about work and sharing family news. At one point, according to the story folks still tell, a man named Ben Peters brought up the business of the old French cemetery nearby. Many people already believed that the spirits of the dead weren't exactly resting in peace there. So, when Peters said that he had seen a big fiery ball of light drifting over the graveyard, no one was too surprised. No one, that is, except MacIntyre.

Still a relative newcomer, MacIntyre hadn't heard all the rumours about the strange goings-on in the cemetery. And even if he had, he probably wouldn't have believed them. Silly superstitions about the dead didn't frighten him, and he made it clear that evening that he wasn't about to be spooked by tales like the one Peters had just told. But the other men were. Peters' description of the eerie light floating over the graves had sent chills down their spines.

Still, they didn't want to look like cowards in front of MacIntyre. So, instead of admitting they were afraid, they decided to dare him to prove that he wasn't. If, as he claimed, there were only dried out, silent, unmoving bones in the cemetery, then he shouldn't be afraid to spend some time there at night.

MacIntyre said he wasn't the least bit frightened to take their dare. In fact, he added, he'd do it that very night. To make sure he really went, one man grabbed a pitchfork leaning against the wall and handed it to MacIntyre. He told MacIntyre to jam it into the ground in the middle of the graveyard. The men agreed that if they found it there the next day, they'd give MacIntyre a large pouch of tobacco. Saying he looked forward to filling his pipe with his prize, MacIntyre headed out into the darkness, pitchfork in hand.

The next day, a few of the men set out for the cemetery. On the way, they passed MacIntyre's place. They called out to him, but the only answer they got was the noise of hungry farm animals waiting to be fed. MacIntyre wasn't there, and he hadn't been there earlier either, or he would have fed his livestock. Nervously, the men continued on their way, grateful that the sun was still high in the sky. When they got close to the cemetery, they called out MacIntyre's name again.

The silence that greeted them there left them cold. But the sight that awaited them up ahead was far more chilling than they could ever have imagined. It was the pitchfork handle that drew them further into the graveyard. It was sticking straight out of the earth, as if marking the spot beneath. And as they drew closer, they saw what was under it.

There, lying on an old grave, was MacIntyre. His eyes were wide open and his mouth was twisted in fear. The men stumbled towards him, ready to help if they could.

But MacIntyre could not be helped. When one man touched his hand, it was cold and stiff. MacIntyre had been dead for hours, and from the look on his face, it was clear that his had not been a peaceful death. Fighting off the horror swelling inside them, the men bent down to pick up MacIntyre's body, but they couldn't lift it. Only then did they notice that the pitchfork had been driven into MacIntyre's long coat, spread out on the ground beneath him.

Someone — or something — had jammed that pitchfork into the ground after MacIntyre had dropped to the ground. But who? Or what? That's the question some folks still ask over 200 years later.

HOME INVASION

Baldoon, Ontario

When John T. McDonald moved his bride into the house he'd built near his father's, he was looking forward to a happy, peaceful life raising a family there. He planned to keep farming the land he shared with his dad in the little village of Baldoon, not far from what's now Chatham, Ontario. And things went pretty much as planned . . . until 1829. By then, the McDonalds had three children, one still an infant. Jane, a teenaged cousin of John's, was also living with them, helping Mrs. McDonald with the children and the housework. But early in the summer of 1829, the McDonald home began playing host to some very unwelcome guests.

Late one night, Mrs. McDonald awoke to the sound of someone moving around in the kitchen. Frightened, she nudged her husband awake, and they both lay still in their bed, trying to figure out what was happening. The noise grew louder, as if several people were now trudging around outside their door. Then they heard their baby cry. It slept in a tiny room off the kitchen, and its cry was a call to action. McDonald leaped out of bed, and yanked open the door to the kitchen. What he found left him stunned and confused. The room was empty and eerily still.

After comforting the baby, the McDonalds decided to keep quiet about what had happened. And they didn't tell their neighbours about the footsteps they heard marching loudly up to their front door on other nights that summer, or about how, every now and then, some family members sensed an unseen presence following them around the house. The last thing they wanted was to have everyone in Baldoon whispering about their house being haunted. But people started talking openly, not just whispering, when word got out about what happened in the McDonalds' barn later in the fall.

Many of Baldoon's farmers were working together bringing in the last of the harvest, and several young women, including Jane, had gathered in the McDonalds' barn to make straw hats. Suddenly, without warning, a heavy log beam came crashing down to the barn floor not far from the girls. Startled, they regrouped in another part of the barn and went back to their hat-making. Not long after, though, another beam broke loose — and then another.

Unharmed, but frightened, the girls scurried out of the barn and took shelter in the house. Feeling safe in the kitchen, they began to calm down. But not for long. Even though no gunshots rang out, bullets started piercing the windows, leaving small, round holes in the glass. The bullets didn't whiz through the room. They simply fell to the floor after coming through the panes. But the young women feared for their lives. They fled from the house and headed across the fields to another farm.

At first the neighbours didn't believe the girls when they blurted out what had happened. Then a young man who had stopped by the McDonald house looking for Jane showed up. He had noticed the holes in the windows and had gone inside to see what was wrong. He'd seen the bullets on the floor and had slipped one into his pocket. When he pulled it out, the girls' story started to ring true. It also started to spread, and before long, the community of Baldoon was abuzz with reports of the unnatural events taking place at the McDonald house.

Over the next several months, more bullets flew through the windows, then stones and lead sinkers used to hold down fishing nets. The scary incidents usually took place in the afternoon and early evening, so groups of curious neighbours were often on hand to witness them. They saw not just projectiles flying into the house, but also kettles full of boiling water lifting off the hearth, chairs and beds moving as if being pushed around by invisible hands, and knives whipping across the kitchen. Amazingly, though, no one was hurt by any of this, at least not physically.

But the McDonalds were suffering. They could find no sane explanation for what was happening to them, and they no longer felt safe in their home. Desperate, they turned to prayerful priests and ministers, psychic researchers and spell-casting witch-hunters to end their torment, but without success. If anything, things got worse.

Small fires started breaking out all over — in closets, cupboards and corners of every room in the house, and outside in the barn. Family and friends spent long hours on fire-watch duty, rushing to douse the nasty balls of flame whenever they mysteriously flared up.

But one morning, in the fall of 1830, the fires got the better of them. As the McDonalds sat in the kitchen eating breakfast, the house began to fill with smoke. Escaping with just the clothes on their backs, they joined the volunteers who raced over to fight the blaze as soon as they spotted the smoke. But their efforts were in vain. The house was left a blackened, burned-out shell and, not long after that, so was the barn.

The people of Baldoon were quick to help McDonald rebuild, and to let the family stay with them in the meantime. But it seemed as if the unnatural force that had plagued the McDonalds for so long was following them.

The neighbours, fearful of the flash fires and the moving furniture that invaded their homes too, eventually gave up trying to house the unfortunate family. John and his wife moved into a tent, and Jane and the children moved in with John's father, Daniel. But fires broke out in Daniel's house too, and it was only with the help of shifts of watchful neighbours that he prevented his home from being reduced to ashes.

Then, in the spring of 1831, as mysteriously as it had begun, the horror ended.

Years later, neighbours would give statements detailing all they had witnessed in the McDonalds' house and in their own homes. Many of them would also note how calm and happy Jane had been throughout the horrible ordeal. Some students of the paranormal see her behaviour as evidence that a poltergeist — a nasty, disruptive ghost — had been at work in Baldoon. Apparently, poltergeists usually pester people if a young person is around. But what the McDonalds suffered was much more than pestering. It was torture of the worst kind — frightening torment by unknown forces for no reason at all.

ALARMING FIRES

Caledonia Mills, Nova Scotia

Nearly a century after the McDonalds were tormented in Ontario, and more than 1500 kilometres east in Nova Scotia, another family named Macdonald suffered through a similar nightmarish experience.

In the early 1900s Alexander Macdonald, his wife, Janet, and their adopted daughter, Mary Ellen, lived on a farm near Caledonia Mills, about 40 kilometres southeast of Antigonish. Like John McDonald in Baldoon, Alexander Macdonald tried not to let the warning signs that something strange might be happening on the farm worry him.

He was already in his seventies the first time the cows got out of the barn in 1921, so he just figured his gnarled hands weren't tying knots as well as they used to. He simply made sure to tie better knots the next time. But the cows got loose again. And again. Even when he wrapped the ropes tethering the cows around big nails, they still managed to get out of their stalls and wander off. His horse was acting up too. Each morning he'd find it in a stall different from the one he'd locked it in the night before. For two weeks the cows kept escaping and the horse kept switching places. Then, to Macdonald's great relief, these strange goings-on stopped. Later he would look back on them as minor annoyances compared to what he had to cope with in January 1922.

Macdonald could explain away the first fire that started in the early hours of January 6. He didn't discover it until he came downstairs in the morning and found a burned-out hole in the kitchen ceiling above the wood stove. He couldn't understand how, but he decided that glowing cinders from the stove were to blame.

Then he smelled the smoke. Following his nose, he rushed to the living room and found a couch and a chair on fire. He beat out the small blazes, and left the room afraid and confused.

When the fires flared up again three days later, a frantic Macdonald turned to his neighbours for help. Three of them agreed to come over and keep watch with him. That night they beat out or poured water on nearly forty fires in different rooms in the house. Fortunately none of them was hurt because, for no reason they could come up with, the flames were cold.

The fiery flare-ups continued the next day and the day after that. Finally Alexander, Janet and Mary Ellen couldn't take any more. Exhausted, confused and absolutely terrified, they decided to go and stay with neighbours for a while. By then, word of their torment had reached Halifax. Never one to pass up a good story, W. H. Dennis, the editor

Two articles about the Nova Scotia ghost from The New York Times, *March 1922*

SCIENTIST SETS OUT FOR HAUNTED HOUSE

Dr. Prince of New York Reaches Halifax on Way to Antigonish to Solve Ghost.

TO SPEND A WEEK THERE

Carries Bells for Spooks to Ring, Knockers to Rap and Shoes for Them to Dance In.

DR. PRINCE BEGINS HIS WAIT FOR 'GHOST'

Continued from Page 1, Column 7.

accounts of interviews with earlier witnesses. The second was to subject Mr. Whidden's evidence to a long oral examination. The third was to see various parties acquainted with certain aspects of the case, particularly the character of the original witnesses. My present conclusions may be thus summarized:

"As to Mr. Whidden, I have no doubt whatever that his testimony is absolutely truthful that he and Carroll heard sounds of unknown origin and experienced sensations which they described as slaps. It is too early for me to pronounce an opinion regarding the cause

of these experiences. Speaking abstractly, they stand on a higher basis of probability as occult events than do the fires, judging by the evidence in other cases, yet that the fires occurred is without question.

"New light upon the entire matter obviously depends upon recurrence of the phenomena while I am in the house. If nothing happens there will be no data on which to work except past testimony already before the public. But if things do happen I shall study them to the utmost detail with the hope of founding a logical verdict upon them.

"No extravagant expectations should be entertained. I do not expect that I shall witness fires or see vistors. That singular sounds and even physical seisations may be experienced is, judging by other cases known to me personally, not improbable, but nothing whatever may occur, and if anything does it may be quite tame to the average man. On the other hand, if it could be proved that they were not due to physical causes, would be of transcendent significance to science."

...sterious cases ...e has investigated the ... is now trailing, he says, is the most mysterious of them all.

"How thirty-eight fires," he declared, "could break out in one night, as related by six of your prominent citizens, is to me a deep mystery, and I should like to push my way through tonight to this house. I have never felt the same eagerness to solve a mystery as I have this one.

112

of the *Halifax Herald*, ran an article about it. Several weeks later, he sent a reporter named Harold Whidden and a detective named B. O. Carroll to follow up on what had been going on at the Macdonalds' farm.

When they arrived in Caledonia Mills, Alexander agreed to take them to his house and spend the night there with them. Most of the furniture had been moved outside when it caught fire, so when it was time for bed, the three men settled down on a pile of rugs in the dining room, huddled under blankets to keep out the winter chill.

No fires started that night, but what did happen was newsworthy. Carroll heard the thumping sounds and footsteps upstairs first, and when the other two woke up, they heard them too. After a few minutes, the noises moved to the living room. Then an invisible hand smacked Whidden's upper arm and brushed against Carroll's wrist. Even though the noises died down, and no one felt any more ghostly contact, it was all the three men could do to spend the rest of the night in the house.

When Carroll and Whidden reported back to the *Herald*'s editor, Dennis decided to invite an American psychic researcher by the name of Walter F. Prince to investigate the fires further. Prince agreed to come to Nova Scotia. In March 1922, he spent a week interviewing the Macdonalds and their neighbours, and carefully examining the fire-plagued house. Then he gave Dennis a report of his findings, and the *Herald* ran an article based on it.

The Macdonalds were very upset when they read it. Ignoring testimony from several witnesses that their daughter hadn't been anywhere near many of the fires when they broke out, Prince had concluded that Mary Ellen had started the fires, probably unintentionally, while suffering from some sort of mental problem. The elderly couple dismissed the report as sensational speculation. And why not? By then they were living back in their home with their daughter, and their lives were once again peaceful, happy and fire-free.

ICY FLAMES

St. John's, Newfoundland and Labrador

A century-old house off Willicott's Lane in St. John's, Newfoundland, was said to be haunted by mysterious fires, but not the sort that scorch walls or leave curtains in flames. All the fires in this house burned cold.

After its elderly owner died, no one lived in the house for a year or so. But every now and then, passersby would think there must be someone there — because they could see a flickering glow in the window of a room on the second floor.

Worried about the place going up in smoke, they'd go in to have a look around. Each time they'd find the house empty, but they'd also find a fire burning in the fireplace in a second-floor bedroom. Then the fire would go out as mysteriously as it had begun.

Unlike the Caledonia Mills fires, these fires never ignited or scorched anything. But like those fires, these fires had burned cold. After each fireplace flare-up, the stone hearth retained not even a hint of warmth.

TOO CLOSE FOR COMFORT

Thetis Lake, British Columbia

Thetis Lake Park is a nature lover's haven about twelve kilometres west of downtown Victoria on Vancouver Island. Within minutes, anyone wanting a break from fast-paced city life can retreat there to enjoy more leisurely activities such as camping, canoeing, fishing, hiking, swimming and birdwatching. But outrunning nasty monsters? That's not usually high on anyone's list of things-to-do at the beach.

It certainly wasn't what two teenaged boys, Gordon Pike and Robin Flewellyn, had in mind when they headed out to Thetis Lake on August 19, 1972. They were just hanging out on the sandy beach when the water near the shore started to bubble and churn. Then, to their horror, a gurgling, scale-covered, four-legged, web-footed, man-sized creature shot out of the water and headed straight for them. Terrified, the two young men turned and ran to their car, the monster following close behind. For a brief second it actually caught up with them and jabbed one boy's hand with its hideous, spiked head.

Gordon and Robin made it safely to the car and sped off toward the local RCMP station. Once the police officers calmed them down, they listened patiently to the boys. They sounded sincere, and one of them did have a cut on his hand, so the Mounties thought they might be telling the truth. But it wasn't until four days later, when two more people reported seeing a silver-scaled creature with bulging eyes and a spiked, fin-like crown on the top of its head rise up out of Thetis Lake, that they began to seriously investigate Gordon's and Robin's tale of terror. However, after weeks of police work, and with no further reports of sightings that might having provided them with hard evidence of the monster's existence, the Mounties had no choice but to abandon their investigation.

The case of the Thetis Lake monster may be filed away somewhere with other cold cases that most likely will never be solved. The monster doesn't keep popping up the way some other lake monsters do, so nobody is too interested in figuring out what it is, or was. After all, it hasn't made a reported appearance since its dramatic surfacing back in the early 1970s.

But that's probably just as well. Unlike other lake monsters, the creature from Thetis Lake could walk — and even run — on land, and it actually attacked somebody. Who'd want a creature like that hanging out in a park just a few minutes' drive from the heart of a major city? Its possible presence isn't something to promote as a tourist attraction.

THE LIVING DEAD

Wilno, Ontario

The story was chilling . . . Believing that a vampire was stalking the area, some men dug up the coffin of a man they thought was coming back to life each night. When the lid was pried off, the dead man sat up. Instantly, the bravest among them pounced, cutting off his head and quickly reburying his remains. Headless, he could no longer pose a threat to the living . . .

Jan Perkowski, an American university scholar of Slavic languages and literature, included this and other bizarre accounts in a report he released in 1969, after interviewing several unnamed individuals in Wilno, Ontario, a small village just south of the eastern tip of Algonquin Park.

Wilno is the oldest Polish settlement in Canada. In 1859 its first settlers came to the area from the Kaszuby region of northern Poland. The people of Wilno are proud of their heritage. When various mainstream newspapers and sensation-seeking tabloids picked up on Perkowski's report with lurid headlines screaming that vampire beliefs lived on in the Ottawa Valley, the proud people of Wilno were furious. They got even angrier when they learned that the Museum of Man in Ottawa (now called the Canadian Museum of History) had paid Perkowski to do his research as part of its preparations for an exhibition on Slavic culture in Canada. Why, they wanted to know, would the government pay for something that would make them the object of ridicule?

Perkowski stood by his report. He had interview transcripts and completed surveys to back it up. Besides, some reporters wondered, why were there so many white crosses along the roadsides around Wilno, if not to ward off vampires? And why did locals cross themselves whenever they drove past them or through town-line crossroads?

Further research would reveal that the crosses and the custom of making the sign of the cross were rooted in a strong religious faith and dated back to the time when there was no Catholic church nearby and the Polish settlers wanted some outward signs of their beliefs. But that's not the stuff of a big news story; nor was the fact that no reporter was able to find anyone who admitted to having given Perkowski his information.

A local explanation for this was that some folks who wanted to remain anonymous had simply told Perkowski what they thought he wanted to hear so he'd stop pestering them with silly questions. It's also possible that back in the 1960s, a few people still held a faint belief in stories passed down from their ancestors about vampires and keeping them at bay with crosses — and garlic. But the only reason someone in Wilno would hang up garlic these days is to dry it out.

Still, there's one ghost story that persists in the area. It's about a beautiful young woman named Stefania who lived in Wilno long ago. Tragically, she came down with a mysterious illness that left her ranting and feverish. At night she would escape from her father's house and walk through the village, her eyes glowing in the darkness.

After she died, her heartbroken father didn't bury her right away, believing if he left her body outside for a few days, she would be freed of any evil forces that might have possessed her. But overnight her body disappeared. When her father discovered that it was gone, he set out on a frantic search for her remains.

His lifeless body was eventually found lying in the graveyard, but Stefania's was never found. Father and daughter are said to be the two ghostly apparitions that are occasionally seen walking through the cemetery. That's assuming, of course, that they really are dead . . .

BEASTLY ENCOUNTER

Ruby Creek, British Columbia

In 1941 George and Jeannie Chapman were living in the Upper Fraser River Valley near Ruby Creek, about 110 kilometres east of Vancouver. George's work on the railway often took him away from home for a few days, leaving Jeannie to care for their three young children and their garden. The Chapman cabin was tucked into a clearing not far from the river and the railway tracks, and even though there were no neighbours close by, Jeannie felt quite safe staying there without George. But not after a terrifying visitor wandered by one fateful summer day.

It was a sunny afternoon. George was away working, Jeannie was inside preparing food, and the children were outside playing. Suddenly, the eldest boy, nine, burst into the cabin, yelling about a cow roaming around in the bush nearby. Jeannie could tell that her son seemed frightened, so she headed outside with him. When she picked out the shape he was pointing at, she decided it was a big bear that was getting a little too close for comfort. The two younger children were still playing happily in the field near the train tracks. When she yelled at them to come home, they started running back toward her. But at that moment, the dark figure her son had seen emerged from the trees, and Jeannie could see that it wasn't a bear.

The creature was big. More than two metres tall and impressively thick-chested, it walked upright like a human, its unusually long arms swinging at its sides. As it got closer, Jeannie saw that its entire body was covered with long, reddish-brown hair about ten centimetres long, longer over its smallish head. From a distance, its face and hands appeared to be black. She had never seen anything like it, and she wasn't going to let it get anywhere near her children.

Keeping a wary eye on the hairy giant, Jeannie ordered her nine-year-old to fetch a blanket from the cabin. Terrified, he did as he was told. When he brought it out to his mother, she pushed him toward his little brother and sister who were on the verge of panic. Holding the blanket in front of them so the beast couldn't see them — and they couldn't see it — she backed them away from the cabin and herded them across the field and down to the river bank. When she reached the beach, she and the children took off, running as fast as they could toward the settlement at Ruby Creek.

George had returned home around dinnertime to find his woodshed door torn apart, and a large barrel full of fish hauled out from the shed and broken open on the ground. Partially eaten fish were strewn about and, worse still, there were massive footprints in the dirt all around the yard. Heart beating faster, George called out to Jeannie, but she didn't answer. Cautiously, he pushed open the cabin door. It was empty.

George rushed back outside, pausing just long enough to study the footprints. They looked as if they'd been made by something at least as big as a bear, but the markings weren't those of bear paws. They were more human in shape, but they were far too big to have been made by any ordinary man. Then George spotted more footprints leading away from the cabin. Following the trail left by his family, he reached the river and made for Ruby Creek. There he found them staying with a relative, safe but still very upset.

When George decided to bring his family back home the next day, three relatives agreed to return with them. For several days they kept watch while George was at work, but no one saw the hairy giant again. For nearly a week, though, they woke up each morning to find fresh giant footprints in the yard. And on two separate nights, the family's dogs barked and howled for several minutes, disturbed by something lurking outside in the darkness.

No one was hurt and nothing else was damaged, but the stress took its toll on the Chapmans. No longer feeling safe, they finally packed up their belongings and moved out of the cabin for good. Visits from a mysterious creature known locally as the sasquatch had driven them from their home.

GIANT FOOTPRINTS

Schefferville, Quebec

More than fifty years ago, an Innu hunter named John Peastitute who lived near Schefferville, Quebec, returned home with a tale so strange not even his family and friends were willing to check it out.

Peastitute was out hunting when he came across some huge footprints. The tracks looked human in shape, but they were so large that no person could have made them. Peastitute bent down and laid his left arm into one to get a rough measure of how long it was. Amazed, he found that the track was longer than his forearm. In fact, it was even longer than his gun.

Peastitute could see that the footsteps led off toward a small mountain, but he resisted the temptation to explore them any further, at least not when he was alone. Instead, he went home and told his grandfather and others what he had seen. But he couldn't convince any of them to go back with him and see the tracks for themselves.

That night one of Peastitute's arms started to hurt and swell up for no apparent reason. The next day, just as mysteriously, it shrank back down to its normal size. The arm that had grown so big and sore had been his left one, the one he had laid in the gigantic footprint.

A BAD OMEN

Toronto, Ontario

Mother Shipton, if she ever existed, was known as a famous prophetess who lived in England in the 16th century. She was supposed to have made many predictions about major events that eventually did happen. When a collection of her predictions was published in the late 1600s, her reputation spread to Europe and beyond.

A new edition of the collection that came out in 1862 boosted her fame in the United States and Canada too. It included more details of Shipton's life, as well as sayings and predictions that hadn't appeared in print before.

Several years later, Richard Head, the editor of the 1862 book, would admit that most of the Mother Shipton story was a hoax, and that he had simply made up the new predictions to increase book sales. But in 1881 one of the scary prophecies worried a lot of people who had no idea that it was one of his fake creations. When it appeared in print, it quickly became the most famous of all of Shipton's rhyming sayings. Just two lines long, it was horrifyingly specific:

The world to an end shall come
In eighteen hundred and eighty-one.

So, as the weeks and months of 1881 slipped away, people who believed in Mother Shipton's ability to foretell the future became more and more worried. And on September 5, 1881, when the colour of the sky changed suddenly and without warning, many of them were absolutely terrified.

The spectacular transformation was like nothing anyone had seen before. In the Toronto area the sky was filled with an orange glow so brilliant that *The Globe* newspaper would report the next day, "The streets and buildings wore an orange tint (and) nearly everything looked as though viewed through an orange glass." By dinnertime, with spectacular swaths of red added to the canvas, the sky looked as if it were on fire. At the same time, darkness seemed to be settling over the city much earlier than it should have.

In communities 200 kilometres to the west, and a few hours earlier, the transformation had been reversed. The darkness came first. In a matter of minutes, the sun seemed to disappear and day was turned into night. Frightened and confused, some people lit lamps and huddled indoors; others ventured out into the dark streets, gazing upwards with neighbours and strangers and worriedly discussing what was happening. Occasional flashes of lightning and cracks of thunder added to a sense of impending doom. As the afternoon wore on, the sky

Mother Shipton

From an Original Picture in the Possession of Ralph Ouseley Esq.ʳ

Pub.ᵈ April 30 1804 by R.S Kirby London House Yard & J Scott 447 Strand

An illustration of Mother Shipton published in 1804

gradually lightened, bringing some sense of relief. But then, as dramatically as it had in Toronto, it began to glow red and continued to do so well into the night.

The next morning those who had managed to sleep woke up to find that all was well in the heavens again. But in some places west of Toronto near Lake Huron they also woke up to find everything outside covered in a black layer of ashes thickened by a brief rainfall that had occurred overnight. The explanation for what had caused the incredible transformation the day before was to be found in those ashes. Dense clouds of smoke and ash from forest fires raging during the unusually dry, hot summer had drifted across Lake Huron and over parts of Ontario, blocking out the sun in some places and bending the sun's rays in others to produce sunset-like displays of red and orange.

But Mother Shipton's believers didn't know this on September 5, 1881. And they didn't know then that a book editor had made up her prediction about the end of the world. So, terrified by what was happening, many of them turned to prayer, convinced that the end was at hand.

MARY RUTHERFORD'S GRAVE

Hanover, Ontario

It's a sad story, the story of Mary Rutherford, and scary too. It may not be true, but that doesn't stop people from telling it. No one knows how or why it began, but over the years its strands have been woven into a spine-tingling tale that can still send a group of teenagers, usually boys, scrambling out of the cemetery as fast as their Nikes can carry them.

The cemetery they run from is an old one in West Bentinck, near Hanover, Ontario. It's where Mary Rutherford's grave is supposed to be, off by itself on a hill toward the back of the property.

But the inscription on the solitary headstone says that Isabella, not Mary, Rutherford was buried there in 1872, when she was seventy-two years old. Further research shows that Isabella married happily and had children and grandchildren. Would there be any reason for her ghost to be haunting this spot? Not likely. But what if Mary Rutherford really is buried on the hill? The spirit of someone who suffered as she did might very well linger in the area.

Mary Rutherford is said to have died when she was still in her thirties. Long after her friends had married and settled down to a happy life raising a family, she finally met the man of her dreams. Thrilled, she planned her wedding. But when the big day arrived, she was left standing alone before the preacher. Her bridegroom had skipped town the night before. Overcome by shame and heartbreak, and still wearing her wedding dress, Mary hanged herself.

Even though her death was a suicide, she was buried in the cemetery — but off by herself on the hill, wearing her wedding dress and lying face down in her coffin. Her spirit, though, couldn't find peace, and her ghost, perhaps still waiting for her lover, appears there to this day . . .

This is the story that, every now and then, draws a small group of young people to the graveyard late at night. One of them issues an "I dare you . . . " challenge, and off they go. What's there to be afraid of? After all, the name on the gravestone they're going to spend time near says "Isabella," not "Mary," so the young buried bride story can't possibly be true, can it? But when they reach their spooky destination under cover of darkness, only the bravest among them dares to touch the headstone — defying the claim that if you do, you'll break a bone in the future.

And if they see it — the wispy glow that appears on the side of the hill, or the shadowy, shimmering figure of a woman moving through the trees — their bravery slips away, and so do they, back to the safety of their homes. Every now and then, a few weeks later, if one of them breaks an arm, or a leg, or even just a big toe, they all remember the night they spent at the graveyard, checking out the tragic tale of Mary Rutherford.

THE COFFIN CAME BACK

Prince Edward Island

Like the Mary Rutherford story, the tale of Charles Coghlan's coffin is creepy — suggesting some supernatural force at work. How else could the casket containing Coghlan's body drift all the way from the Gulf of Mexico and end up, eight years after his death, in Prince Edward Island, a place he had said he would never return to?

The story has been around since the early twentieth century. It appeared in an early *Ripley's Believe It or Not* column, and was featured in the first *Believe It or Not* book Robert Ripley published in 1929. After that it spread around the world and eventually became one of Ripley's most famous and popular reports of incredible events.

At its core, Coghlan's story is a familiar one . . .

A young man born in the 1840s in an isolated farming

community — in this case, in Prince Edward Island — has a dream: he wants to become an actor. His father warns him that if he leaves to follow his dream, he'll never be welcomed back by his family. He leaves anyway, vowing never to return to his birthplace. He becomes a successful actor in England and eventually ends up performing in the United States with a touring company. On November 27, 1899, while appearing in a play in Galveston, Texas, he drops dead on the stage, and is buried in a local cemetery. In September 1900, a powerful hurricane hits Galveston Island and surging waters unearth his coffin and wash it out to sea. Over the next eight years, currents carry it out of the Gulf of Mexico, around the southern tip of Florida, up the Atlantic, around Nova Scotia and into the Gulf of St. Lawrence, where it finally washes ashore on Prince Edward Island. A metal plate found inside the casket has Coghlan's name on it. The young man with a dream has finally come home.

Folklore researchers at the University of Prince Edward Island say the story is a myth, and they're probably right. Coghlan wasn't laid to rest in P.E.I., and he wasn't born there. Some sources state that he was born in Paris, France, in 1841, but he grew up in Ireland and was known as an Irish actor. He did spend some time in P.E.I. While touring the United States in the late 1880s, he visited the island and liked it so much he rented an old farmhouse at Abells Cape, near the Fortune River, and lived in it for a few years.

Coghlan did pass away in Galveston on November 27, 1899, but he didn't die on stage. He had been sick for a few weeks by then, and an understudy was playing his part that night. Galveston newspapers reported his death, along with his wife's plans to have his body taken by train to New York to be cremated. But that's where the case goes cold.

Years later a fire destroyed the records of the funeral home that had held on to his remains until his wife had finished making arrangements to move his body. So it looks as though no one will ever know for certain exactly what did happen to Coghlan's coffin. Maybe that's why some people still want to believe that it eventually carried Charles Coghlan, actor, back to the beauty and peace of Prince Edward Island.

MURDER MOST FOUL

Regina, Saskatchewan

Occasionally security monitors at 1925 Victoria Avenue in downtown Regina, Saskatchewan, indicate that someone is moving around on the third floor, even though there's no one up there. At least not anyone alive.

For some people who work in the building, the fact that a monitor can detect the mysterious movement is proof that they weren't just imagining things when they saw the young woman with glowing red hair drifting through the third floor rooms. They figure she's also the one who turns the lights on and off up there.

There's a restaurant on the main floor of 1925 Victoria now, but the whole building used to be home to a posh private men's club called the Assiniboia Club. The fine old building has been completely renovated, so the club now

The Assiniboia Club in Regina, Saskatchewan

occupies just the top two floors.

There are female members of the club now too. The rules banning them were dropped in 1988. But decades ago, when women weren't even supposed to enter the building, some young ladies did get in, slipping in through a side door and up the stairs to private rooms on the third floor. Members in town on business could stay in those rooms overnight instead of checking in to a hotel at the end of a long working day. But some of the men would sneak female companions upstairs — and it's said that the ghost who haunts the Assiniboia Club was one of those young women.

The story explaining her lingering presence tells of her coming often to visit one particular member. Over time she fell in love with him. When she let him know how she felt, he told her he didn't want to have anything more to do with her. But she didn't want to stop seeing him.

Some say the man was afraid she would cause him all sorts of trouble. Whatever the reason, he's supposed to have arranged to have her murdered at the club.

After she was axed to death, her lover and a few other members organized the removal and disposal of her body. But not even death could keep her away from the club. For more than half a century she has been returning to the third floor. But why? Is she reaching out across time seeking revenge? Or justice? Or is she looking for a love lost so long ago?

THE LADY VANISHES

Kingston, Ontario

A ruthless boyfriend is also said to be behind the gruesome death of a young woman whose presence haunts the 300-block of King Street East in historic downtown Kingston, Ontario. Unlike the anonymous member of the Assiniboia Club, this fellow has a name: John Napier.

According to one of the best-known tales of haunting in the Kingston area, back in 1868 Napier had a girlfriend named Theresa Beam. One night he arranged a secret rendezvous with her in a laneway off King Street. But when the couple met, instead of sharing hugs and kisses, they got into a terrible fight that ended with Napier strangling Theresa with his bare hands. Then, to hide his crime, he buried her body nearby, or so the story goes.

Over the years, people have reported seeing a short,

attractive woman in a long, black old-fashioned dress moving mysteriously around the neighbourhood. When anyone tries to speak with her, she vanishes.

And in the 1970s a photographer who was renting a studio at 348 King Street East was so bothered by spooky knocks — usually three in a row — that he and his assistant finally used a ouija board to try and find out what was going on. They claimed to have connected with Theresa's spirit and learned that she was the source of the strange noises. The spirit also led them to believe that her remains were buried in the basement, and that she had been restless ever since her death because she wasn't buried in holy ground.

Another tenant was also bothered by unexplained knocks and noises and, familiar with the photographer's story, had the cellar floor dug up, but found no buried bones. When more work was done on the basement a few years later, a construction crew uncovered a boarded-up passageway leading next door to 350 King. Maybe Beam's body is buried in its cellar. After all, the buildings are connected.

But digging up a basement is an expensive project, and most people, including the owners of 350 King, don't want to spend a lot of money chasing a ghost. So neither Theresa Beam's remains nor her story have been put to rest — yet.

Ouija, The Talking Board

In 1890, when trying to make contact with the spirit world was quite the fad, Elijah Bond of Baltimore, Maryland, invented an alphabet-covered board that he claimed would give an "intelligent answer to any question." The board came with a pointer on little legs. When players lightly rested their fingers on it, it was supposed to answer questions by sliding to the words YES or NO, and to letters that would spell out names and other words. Bond and two partners formed the Kennard Novelty Company, called the invention the Ouija board (a combination of the French and German words for "yes") and started marketing it as a parlour game.

The board was a hit.

One of Elijah Bond's original Ouija boards

In 1901, William Fuld took over the company and he, and then his children, mass-produced Ouija boards until Parker Brothers bought them out in 1966.

Parker Brothers and several other companies are still selling Ouija boards today, and there are still some people who believe the boards can answer their questions and help them connect with the spirits of people who've died.

They might change their minds, though, if they tried using the board blindfolded, with someone else writing down the letters the pointer moves to. When they take the blindfolds off, they might be surprised to see the nonsense words the Ouija board has come up with. It might leave them wondering if it's just a game.

That's all it is . . . isn't it?

SCHOOL SPIRIT

Edmonton, Alberta

A Ouija board may be just a game, but Ron Hlady believed it helped him make sense of the weird experiences he had to put up with while working as a caretaker at the Edmonton Public Schools Archives and Museum in the 1980s.

The museum is located in the old McKay Avenue School, in a part of Edmonton that dates back to the city's early days. And for many years, Hlady and others have felt that spirits from the past were still present in the museum. How else to explain things like voices in empty rooms, locked doors being unlocked by invisible hands, pictures being taken down from walls, and blinds being ripped off windows? Hlady turned to a Ouija board for an answer.

In an article he wrote for an Edmonton newspaper,

Hlady said that the spirit of a construction worker named Peter was haunting the building. He had fallen to his death while working on an addition to the school site back in 1912. But how could Peter have "told" him all this through a game board? Maybe that's the question someone should ask the Ouija board.

The McKay Avenue School in Edmonton, Alberta

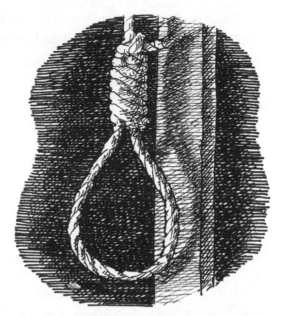

THE FUGITIVE'S GHOST

London, Ontario

There are strange sounds heard in the old courthouse in London, Ontario. There are also areas that suddenly become icy cold. It's said that these mysterious occurrences are the work of the ghost of Peg-Leg Brown, who was hanged in the yard outside the jail on May 17, 1899.

Peg-Leg's real name was Marion Brown. He was a young cowboy from Texas who had lost his left leg while trying to hitch a ride on a slow-moving freight train. By the time he was in his twenties, he had earned a reputation as a thief and a troublemaker who wasn't afraid to use the revolver he always carried. On the run from the law in the United States in the late 1890s, he worked his way north and eventually crossed the border into Canada.

On the morning of June 24, 1898, Brown beat up a

railway worker who tried to stop him from tramping along the train tracks in London. When the attack was reported to police, officers on patrol went looking for a man with a wooden "peg" leg, last seen wearing a large, floppy black hat. Constable Michael Toohey, a young father of three, spotted the culprit on a city street late that evening. When he tried to arrest the suspect, the man pulled out a revolver and fired two shots. The second one was fatal. Then the killer limped off into the darkness, his black hat lying in the dirt as evidence to the vicious, senseless crime.

The cross-border manhunt that followed lasted nearly four months. More than forty one-legged men who roughly matched Peg-Leg's description were arrested, and then released when they were able to prove their innocence. Finally, though, Brown was tracked down near Seattle, Washington, and, according to many lawyers, illegally brought back to Canada to stand trial. To make sure he couldn't escape during his long journey east to London, guards confiscated his wooden leg.

Brown's capture, jury trial and a conviction based on rather skimpy circumstantial evidence all made the headlines. Brown maintained his innocence to the end, but when a judge sentenced him to hang for killing Toohey, crowds outside the London courthouse cheered. They were also ready to cheer when they lined up to witness his execution on the morning of May 17, 1899, but most of them weren't allowed inside the jail yard where the scaffold had been built.

Brown prayed quietly as he climbed the scaffold steps, and he didn't resist when the hangman slipped the noose over his head and tightened it around his neck. But as the trap door opened and he fell to his death, a huge flash of lightning pierced the morning sky, followed by an ear-splitting clap of thunder. At the same time, the minister who had stood near Brown to comfort him cried out, "Oh, God forgive us. Oh, God, forgive our country."

The eerie circumstances surrounding Brown's death led to all sorts of strange stories of his returning to haunt the courthouse jail. Over the years, guards would warn rowdy prisoners that his ghost would spend the night with them if they didn't settle down. It was also reported that shortly before he died, Brown had claimed that no grass would ever grow over his grave, and none ever did. Brown's body was buried in the jail yard, which was eventually paved over. In 1985 construction crews working there dug up the remains of a one-legged man identified as Brown. Only then was his body laid to rest in a lawn-covered church cemetery.

But if Brown's spirit finally found peace there, why do some people still feel a ghostly presence in the old courthouse, or hear a peg leg tap-tapping across the floor, especially on May 17, the anniversary of Brown's execution?

The old courthouse in London, Ontario

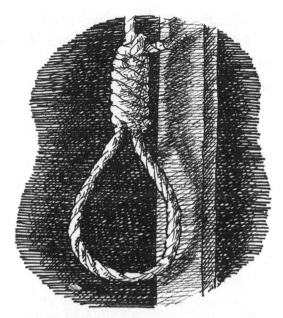

POSTSCRIPT TO A HANGING

Prince Edward County, Ontario

In the late 1880s, a bungled robbery on a farm in Prince Edward County, east of Belleville, Ontario, led to the killing of a man named Peter Lazier. Clear bootprints in the snow led to the arrest and eventual murder conviction of two men from the Sandbanks area, George Louder and Joseph Tompsett.

Right to the end, both men said they weren't guilty, and some folks believed that Tompsett might not be. But in June 1884, the two were hanged, back to back, in the yard of the Picton courthouse. The execution was especially gruesome, with both men taking several minutes to die.

Afterwards, rumours spread that one of the sets of incriminating bootprints had been made by another person. A man who was suspected of knowing what had really happened swore that he did not. He protested that if he were lying, God would make him go bald. According to a story told locally, within a few weeks the man started losing all the hair on his face and head.

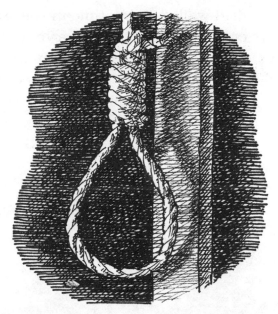

VICTORIA'S MOST HAUNTED

Victoria, British Columbia

Chains rattling and footsteps shuffling in empty alleys . . . an invisible cigar smoker puffing away in a no-smoking restaurant . . . a pub owner murdered a century ago sitting at the bar of a fancy hotel . . .

It's no wonder that Bastion Square in Victoria, British Columbia, is said to be the most haunted place in the province. Ghosts have visited most of the buildings along its cobblestone walkway, and the Maritime Museum has had more than its share of spectral guests. It's located in the city's first courthouse, built on the site of the city's first jail after it was torn down. In the second half of the nineteenth century, criminals sentenced to death were hanged in the jail yard.

Part of the square also served as a graveyard for several

prisoners who died while serving time in the jail.

These days crowds of tourists are drawn to the square's stylish shops and charming cafés, and many businesses have opened offices in its attractively restored buildings.

But the many otherworldly apparitions that both tourists and workers have seen or heard serve as ghostly reminders of the darker history of Bastion Square.

Bastion Square in Victoria, B.C.

THE SCHOONER CAPTAIN'S SPECTRE

Tobermory, Ontario

For centuries, lights shining from shore have guided sailors through the blackness of night to safety.

Since 1858 the Cove Island lighthouse near Tobermory, Ontario, has served as such a beacon, marking safe passage through the dangerous waters of the main channel between Lake Huron and Georgian Bay. Until it was automated in 1991, keepers living on the island maintained its light in brilliant working order. But there was nothing keeper George Currie could do to help Amos Tripp, captain of the schooner *Regina*, as he struggled to keep his small sailing ship afloat on a stormy autumn evening in 1881.

Battered by gale-force winds and swamped by huge waves, the *Regina* was in danger of breaking apart. When Tripp realized that he wouldn't be able to manoeuvre it

153

through the strait, he decided to try and aim it right at Cove Island's sandy beach. He figured that if he grounded the ship on the soft sand, it might survive the storm. What happened next will never be known for certain.

Later, crew members would report that Tripp had ordered them into the lifeboat, but the *Regina* began taking on water so quickly that he couldn't get off before it sank. Some locals who knew Tripp well didn't believe that version of events, and they wondered aloud if the sailors had refused to obey his order to make for the beach and had abandoned him and the ship. Whatever the truth was, three facts were certain: the sailors escaped from the *Regina*, the schooner sank and Amos Tripp drowned. The crew rowed through the stormy night and finally made it safely to the village of Lion's Head, nearly a hundred kilometres from Cove Island.

Back on the island, lightkeeper Currie didn't learn that the *Regina* had sunk until a sailor dropped anchor a few days later and told him about the tragic fate of the schooner and its captain. Knowing that, Currie was saddened, but not too surprised, to find Tripp's body washed up on shore two weeks later. The keeper wrapped the corpse in sailcloth and buried it in a shallow grave until news of its whereabouts got back to the mainland and a tugboat captain came to collect it for a proper burial in Collingwood.

But Captain Tripp may not have left the island for good. Over the years, a few keepers reported an eerie feeling of being watched as they went about their tasks. Every now and then they also noticed that the captain's invisible hand had done some of the tasks involved in caring for the lighthouse. And according to one story, when a lax keeper dozed off, Tripp's ghostly presence relit the light when it flickered out.

When the lighthouse was automated in 1991, the last official lightkeeper left Cove Island. But kayakers and boaters still tell of seeing a dark figure on the beach. It's a lonely place to be, especially at night, but perhaps Captain Tripp still feels safe at home there.

KEEPER OF THE LIGHT

Toronto, Ontario

The Cove Island lighthouse looks out over the windswept waters of Lake Huron. Stunningly beautiful, but desolate too, it's the perfect setting for ghostly appearances by a schooner captain who went down with his ship nearby.

But why would a ghost be haunting a lighthouse on a cottage-dotted island just a few minutes ferry ride from downtown Toronto?

The Gibraltar Point lighthouse on what's now called Centre Island was built in 1808 to mark the safe entrance into Toronto's harbour. A six-sided stone structure that stood sixteen metres high, it was topped by a light burning so brightly that on a clear night it could be seen from a distance of several kilometres. The original lamp was fuelled by whale oil. Climbing the tower's seventy steps to light it — and keeping it burning — was the job of the lighthouse's first keeper, John Paul Rademuller.

Rademuller worked at Gibraltar Point from 1809 to 1815. He lived in a small keeper's house built near the lighthouse. At the time, the point was at the end of a long, sandy peninsula connected to the mainland. Until a fierce storm in 1858 washed away parts of that narrow spit of land, leaving behind the Toronto islands, people could actually walk or ride a horse over to the point. It was also just a short rowboat ride away from the bustling new city taking shape across the harbour. So it wasn't unusual for visitors to drop in on Rademuller, a kind and friendly man.

It's not known if friends or strangers were at the lighthouse on January 2, 1815. In fact, there's very little information about what actually happened on that fateful day. But, according to one short item in the *York Gazette* two weeks later, Rademuller was murdered on the evening of January 2 in a "most barbarous and inhuman" way.

The most popular version of events surrounding his death has two or three soldiers showing up at his place for the bootlegged liquor he was rumoured to be getting from smugglers from the United States. Either he had none, or he refused to give it to them. Enraged, the soldiers killed him, chopped up his body, and buried his remains some distance from the lighthouse.

Another version hints at an evening of drinking and card playing ending in a fatal fight, with the frightened killers getting rid of the body because they figured no one would believe that they hadn't intended to kill Rademuller.

Still another, perhaps less likely, version has the keeper being chased up the seventy steps to the lamp room where he was hit on the head with a rock, dragged outside, and tossed to the ground below. This last scenario might

157

explain why some people have heard mysterious footsteps on the stairs spiralling to the top of the tower. Then again, they might just be the sounds of Rademuller continuing to do his job. A few visitors have reported seeing his ghost doing exactly that.

Maybe it was because Rademuller's body wasn't found that no one was ever punished for his murder. The *York Gazette* article concerning his death did refer to some suspects being in jail. A few months later, though, the same paper ran a couple of lines saying that there'd been

The Gibraltar Point Lighthouse at night

no conviction of the supposed murderers. But there's no record of a trial ever being held, so mystery surrounds the case to this day.

In 1893 George Durnan, lighthouse keeper from 1853 to 1908, and his uncle, Joseph Durnan, came across parts of a coffin and a few skeletal remains buried in the sand about 150 metres west of the keeper's house. Although there was no proof that the remains were those of Rademuller, people assumed that they were. The location of the grave fit so well with stories about where he had been buried.

If the bones were in fact Rademuller's, their discovery didn't seem to put his spirit to rest. Maybe his ghostly presence lingers on, waiting for justice. Or could it be that he loved his job so much that he just couldn't bear to bid a final farewell to Gibraltar Point?

The plaque on the lighthouse wall

GHOST ON THE MOVE

Halifax, Nova Scotia

For generations the ghost of a young soldier named Alexander Alexander, nicknamed Double Alex, haunted the Sambro Island lighthouse guarding the entrance to Halifax Harbour. He would be seen wandering the beach and heard moving around the lighthouse. He was also blamed for unexplained knocks on the keeper's house door, and for items being mysteriously moved from where they'd been left.

Back in the 1830s, Alexander was one of a small group of soldiers stationed on the island to maintain the lighthouse. According to locals who have passed down his story, he headed off to the mainland for some fun. After spending army funds on a week of heavy drinking, he managed to make it back to Sambro, afraid of what would happen because he had spent all the money, and suffering from a huge hangover. When his captain refused to give him a shot of rum to help ease his pain, he stumbled off and hanged himself in an outbuilding. He was still breathing when fellow soldiers found him and cut him down, but they were too late to save him.

In 1998, with the lighthouse fully automated, the last of the keepers moved off the island, and Alex wasn't seen or heard from again — at least not on Sambro.

But after the Maritime Museum of the Atlantic in Halifax displayed an old lens that had been used to focus the beacon shining brightly from Sambro Island, windows started breaking in the museum for no reason. The cause was clear to some workers there. Double Alex had moved to the mainland.

CLOSE ENCOUNTER IN COTTAGE COUNTRY

Huntsville, Ontario

Whenever he could, Oscar Magosci would drive up from Toronto to a cottage lot he owned near Huntsville, Ontario. He loved camping out there, and would spend many evenings lying on a ridge beside a flickering campfire, staring up at the night sky. That's what he was doing two days into his vacation in the summer of 1975 when he spotted the flashing orange light silently zigzagging across the star-filled sky.

As a boy growing up in Hungary, Magosci had been fascinated by "flying saucers." He had kept up his interest in the subject when he immigrated to Canada in 1957, and never passed up an opportunity to gaze at the stars. This wasn't the first time he had observed a UFO (unidentified flying object), but the orange orb was unlike anything he had seen in the past, and it appeared to be getting closer and closer.

Magosci's heart began to beat faster. The night before, he had been struck by a powerful feeling that he was about to encounter something from outer space. That premonition might become a reality. The strange object was now close enough for Magosci to see that it was disc-shaped, not round. Briefly, it disappeared from view, but suddenly reappeared about 100 metres away, hovering just above the trees. Magosci stood still in the dark, watching as the orange glow began to pulse — brighter, dimmer, brighter, dimmer. The effect was hypnotic. After about ten minutes, the large shape took on a greenish glow, rose up, glided overhead and disappeared beyond the ridge where Magosci was camped.

The urge to see where it had gone was irresistible. With the help of his flashlight, Magosci worked his way down the ridge and along an old dirt road. He found what he was searching for in a clearing off to one side. What looked to him like a flying saucer, about ten metres across and near-ly three metres deep, was hovering just above the ground. Then, slowly and silently, it landed. Excited beyond belief, but frightened too, Magosci waited several minutes before feeling brave enough to approach the mysterious craft and touch it. It felt warm.

In *My Space Odyssey in UFOs*, a book he published five years after his amazing encounter, Magosci described in detail how he struggled to find the courage to step through a door-like opening that parted before him, and how he stayed inside an eerily lit chamber for some time before exiting and watching it lift off and disappear. As a believer in alien life and exploratory voyages from outer space, he was far calmer and braver than most people would be in

A UFO sighting over Hamilton, Ontario, in 1975

such a situation. But he also described being absolutely terrified at one point, in the moments after he had stepped aboard and the door slid shut behind him.

Magosci concluded that the spaceship was some sort of unmanned robotic vehicle of unknown origin — a true UFO. But one can't help thinking, as Magosci did, about what might have happened if that door had never slid open again.

ALIEN SIGNALS

Toronto, Ontario

Even after Oscar Magosci wrote a book about his UFO experiences, most people didn't believe his story. They were even less willing to believe a Toronto-area woman named Betty Stewart Dagenais. She claimed to have suffered through three harrowing abductions by aliens, starting way back in 1925.

In the late 1980s, she met with a Toronto-based team of UFO researchers, headed by Larry Fenwick, to discuss her experiences. During the meeting, she showed them a small lump behind her left ear. She believed something had been implanted there during her third abduction in 1961 because, after that, she began hearing strange sounds or signals. They had faded over the years, but Dagenais figured an alien transmitter was still inside her and she wanted it out.

Fenwick agreed to help. He arranged for whatever it was to be surgically removed at York County Hospital in 1989, and was on hand with a video camera during the operation. The item that was removed was round, nearly black and very small — just one by one-and-a-half milli-metres. It also looked as if it had once had something very tiny attached in two places.

Dagenais had passed away by the time Fenwick submit-ted her implant to a scientific laboratory in Mississauga, near Toronto, in 1995. An engineer named George Hathaway, another member of the UFO research team, analyzed it carefully using a scanning electron micro-scope. He didn't figure out what it was, but his analysis showed that it contained mainly aluminum, titanium and silicon, as well as trace amounts of calcium, potassium, sodium, sulphur, iron and chlorine. These elements can also be found in bits of ordinary rock lying around outside. But a few of them, especially titanium and aluminum, can be used to make probes and transmitters . . .

WİTHOUT A TRACE

Duncan, British Columbia

It's easy to see why Chris Rutkowski — writer, TV producer, media specialist and UFO researcher from Winnipeg, Manitoba — would include the disappearance of Granger Taylor in his "top eleven" list of strange UFO reports.

Taylor lived in Duncan, British Columbia. He had two passions in life — a love of machinery and an obsession with UFOs. He left school when he finished Grade 8 to become a mechanic's apprentice, and quickly earned a reputation as a real whiz when it came to repairing any and every kind of machine that needed fixing. He also loved building replicas of things such as planes and cars, and rescuing abandoned machines, including an old train locomotive that he pieced back together in the early 1970s when he was still in his teens. And, in pursuit of his other passion, he built a flying saucer in his parents' backyard.

Taylor fashioned the main shell of his spacecraft out of two large satellite dishes, anchored to a base with legs to keep it off the ground. He furnished it much as a kid would a tree house, even hauling up an old couch and TV so he could spend time there in comfort. When he wasn't working on some piece of machinery, he could usually be found in it, reading and thinking about how a real spaceship might be made to fly.

But the morning after a powerful thunderstorm rolled across Vancouver Island in November 1980, no one could find Taylor anywhere. He and his pick-up truck had vanished.

Taylor did leave behind a note for his parents, telling them he was going to board an alien ship that would take him on a three-and-a-half-year-long voyage to outer space and back. The police investigation that followed his disappearance turned up no clues as to what might have happened to him. After three and a half years without any news about or from their son, the Taylors feared the worst. But in the faint hope that he would return one day, they left the red-and-white flying saucer standing in their yard.

CAUSE FOR CONCERN?

Suffield, Alberta

Over the years, concern for the safety of airline passengers has increased. Even before a string of deadly hijackings, both commercial and military pilots had to report any unidentified plane or "flying object" they saw in the sky or picked up on their radar systems. In the new millennium, doing this has become more important than ever.

On March 21, 2004, the pilot of a Challenger jet flying over Suffield, Alberta, radioed air traffic controllers in Edmonton to say he could see a very bright light falling from the sky, trailing smoke behind it. Two other pilots filed similar reports at about the same time.

Later the pilots, and several other people who observed the incredibly bright orb in the early evening sky that Sunday, would learn that what they'd seen was an asteroid, or chunk of comet, burning up as it entered Earth's atmosphere.

But when he first spotted the unidentified object not far from his plane, the Challenger's pilot must have felt a brief moment of extra concern for the welfare of his passengers — and rightly so. Security worries are always greater if one has an important world leader on board, and that evening the pilot was flying Paul Martin, Canada's prime minister, to a meeting with farmers near Picture Butte, Alberta. The last thing the pilot needed to worry about during that flight was a UFO.

ARCTIC ENCOUNTER

Northwest Territories

Apparently, Prime Minister Martin wasn't aware that he'd just had a close encounter with a UFO in March, 2004. But Vera Ovayuak, of Tuktoyaktuk, Northwest Territories, was very aware of her much closer encounter seven years earlier, on February 22, 1997.

It was early in the morning, and Ovayuak, her son Grant, Lena Kotokak, and Churchill and Dorothy Wolki were driving a truck along the ice road that links "Tuk" and Aklavik in the winter.

Suddenly Ovayuak spotted a large silver-coloured shape drifting across the road just above the trees. Then, as the mysterious flying object landed gently near the road, another one appeared out of nowhere and touched down a bit further back of the first one. Ovayuak and the others could see that the craft closer to the truck had four large windows, each one lit up with a bright blue glow.

Curious, but nervous too, the five travellers decided to keep driving.

But panic quickly replaced any curiosity they might have felt when the ships rose up and seemed to start following them. For more than ten minutes the blue-lit crafts glided just above the ground behind the truck. Then, as suddenly as the UFOs had appeared, they were gone.

Relieved, the Ovayuaks and their neighbours drove on in silence, each one trying to make sense of what they had just seen.

THE LURE OF THE FALLS

Niagara Falls, Ontario

Sometimes a person who's still very much alive haunts a place with his or her disturbing behaviour. Francis Abbott, the mysterious young Englishman who came to be known as the Hermit of Niagara, was just such a person.

Niagara Falls had already become a famous tourist attraction when Abbott appeared there in June 1829. Visitors from across North America and abroad were coming to marvel at the world wonder they had heard so much about. For many, gazing at the Niagara River racing toward the brink and spilling down into the roaring whirlpool below was — and still is — almost a hypnotic experience. Perhaps, for Abbott, it was.

Abbott stood out when he first showed up in town on the American side of the Falls.

Tall and well-built, he punctuated his long strides with a gentleman's walking cane. He wore a long brown cloak that flowed out behind him as he walked, but his feet were bare. Abbott checked into a single room at a small inn with just a few possessions — a bedroll, a big book, a soft case like those in which artists carried drawing pads and supplies, and a flute.

Planning to stay about a week, Abbott quickly changed his mind. As he explained to the librarian who managed a nearby reading room, he found the combination of the Falls' incredible beauty and terrifying power both overwhelming and irresistible. He had travelled widely across Europe, but had never before been so strongly moved by a place. He wanted to experience the Falls to the full for at least six months, and he wanted to do it alone.

Abbott quickly drew up plans for a little cabin. He wanted to build it on one of the Three Sisters — small islands in the river above the Falls, just south of the much larger Goat Island. The plans included a drawbridge that he could pull up to keep anyone walking around Goat Island at bay. He was refused permission to build on any of the Sisters, but Augustus Porter, Goat Island's owner, said he could stay in a small, existing log cabin on the big island.

Excited, Abbott packed up his flute, a violin he had just bought, and some basic supplies, and headed across the bridge from the U.S. mainland to his new home. Mostly, he kept to himself. At times he wouldn't answer when people tried to speak to him, but he wasn't rude or angry, just silent. He played his flute, his violin and a guitar that he bought later. The haunting strains of his music would drift through the trees until they could no longer be heard above the roar of the Falls. He composed a little music, and he wrote a lot. According to some people, he wrote

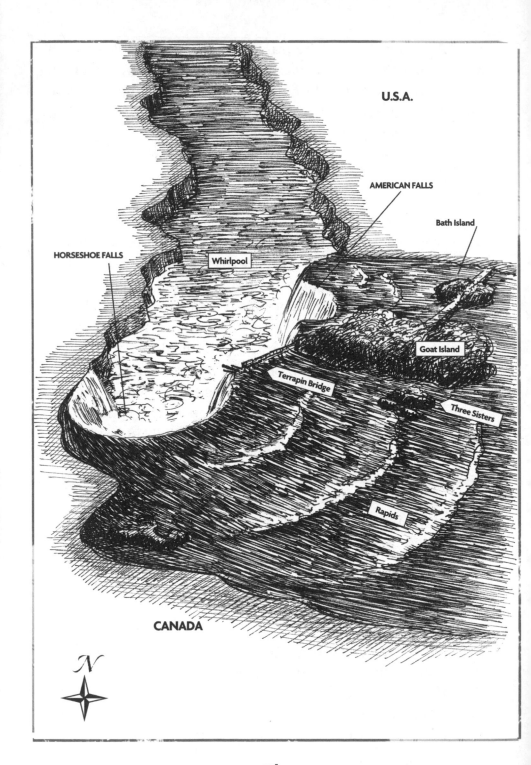

U.S.A.

AMERICAN FALLS

Bath Island

HORSESHOE FALLS

Whirlpool

Goat Island

Terrapin Bridge

Three Sisters

Rapids

CANADA

N

only in Latin, and threw out anything he'd written as soon as he finished it. He got a cat and a dog, and walked with the dog around the island. And whenever the mood struck, and it struck often, he went to the river, getting as close to the rapids and the Falls as possible.

A narrow bridge jutted out from the southwest corner of Goat Island, linking it to a solid pile of large rock known as the Terrapin Rocks. At the end of the bridge there was a thick section of timber that jutted out beyond the rocks above the eastern edge of the Horseshoe Falls on the Canadian side of the river.

Only the most daring of tourists walked out on that bridge, and they didn't linger there. Under it the rapids raced toward the edge of the Falls, leaving them trembling with fear at the possibility of the bridge collapsing or of the rails giving way.

That's where Abbott would go to get close to the water. He would walk out on the bridge barefoot, his long hair framing his face. He would cross the bridge and, step by step, walk out on the wooden beam. Some days he would pace back and forth on it for hours. Occasionally he would stand perfectly still on it, balanced on one foot, or sit on it, his legs swinging over the edge. And sometimes he would go right to the end of the beam, kneel, slip down over the side of it and, holding on with both hands, dangle over the roaring, mist-spewing whirlpool beneath the Horseshoe Falls.

People on the island and at lookout points on the Canadian side of the Falls would cry out in horror, but he seemed to be oblivious to the danger he was in. He once told someone in town that he wasn't doing anything more dangerous than a sailor who climbed high up the rigging of a ship during a storm. He also said that he wanted to rid himself of all fear.

Abbott eventually had to move out of the cabin on Goat Island, but he didn't leave Niagara. He built himself a hut on the American shore near a ferry landing. And every morning, even in the winter when chunks of ice floated by, he would go for a swim in the river.

But one June morning in 1831, two years after he had come to town, he went swimming three times, and the third time, he didn't come back.

A ferry operator who saw him dive in noticed that he seemed to stay underwater for a long time — but he was used to Abbott's strange behaviour. It took him a few minutes to realize that the Englishman had disappeared and to send out a call for a search party.

Abbott's body was swept down the river and over the edge into the whirlpool, and there it stayed. Day after horrifying day, rescuers struggled to reach it as crowds peered through the mist to watch it surface briefly before it was sucked back under the swirling eddies. Finally, after eleven days, it was recovered and buried in Oakwood Cemetery in Niagara Falls, New York.

At last Francis Abbott was free of Niagara's spell. But perhaps the Falls will never quite be free of Abbott's . . .

A LONELY SOUL

Southampton, Ontario

Near the turn of the twentieth century, a hermit lived in a rough shack he had built on a small Lake Huron island near Southampton, Ontario. He foraged for his food, trapping small game on the island and catching fish offshore from a homemade dugout canoe. Some locals say he'd gone there, broken-hearted, after a woman he loved rejected him. Others worried that he was mentally ill, but he kept so much to himself that he wouldn't take help from anyone.

No one knew how long the unfortunate man had been there, and no one knew his name. Because of the strange cries and howling sounds he made, people usually referred to him as "the wild man" and nicknamed Bowes Island, where he lived, Wild Man's Island.

One day, after a spell of rough weather, some fishermen working their nets spotted the hermit's canoe drifting aimlessly on the lake. Cautiously, they rowed over for a closer look. The boat was empty.

The hermit was never seen again, and everyone assumed he had drowned. But every now and then, for several years after he disappeared, someone would hear his haunting cries.

THE HEADLESS NUN

French Fort Cove, New Brunswick

As British soldiers were forcing Acadians (French settlers living in the Maritime provinces) to leave Nova Scotia in 1755, a small group of Acadians living along the Miramichi River east of Chatham, New Brunswick, were getting ready to put up a fight.

They set up camp at French Fort Cove, helping the French soldiers stationed there to reinforce the small fort and stockpile food supplies and ammunition. Then, always keeping a watchful lookout, they went about their daily tasks.

But possible expulsion by the British wasn't the only threat they had to cope with. Leprosy — a terrible, flesh-destroying disease — had infected the community. Those suffering from leprosy had to isolate themselves on a small island nearby.

A nun named Sister Marie Inconnu worked tirelessly around the cove, nursing the sick, caring for the elderly and helping pregnant women deliver their babies. Everyone loved her. So she was the one with whom two widowed women shared a secret. They told her where they had buried the most valuable possessions of their families and friends so soldiers couldn't steal them if the British attacked.

Unfortunately both women became ill and died, and somehow word got out that Sister Marie was the only one left who knew where the treasures were hidden. That's why two men wracked by leprosy attacked her one night as she was crossing the footbridge over a creek running into the cove. Desperate to escape their wretched lives, they were ready to do anything to get enough money to pay a ship's captain to take them far away from the Miramichi.

The men grabbed Sister Marie and demanded that she tell them where the valuables were buried. When she refused, they took turns beating her. Still, she said nothing. Finally, one of the crazed pair drew his sword and sliced off her head. Before he and his partner ran away, leaving Sister Marie's bleeding corpse on the bridge, he picked up the head and threw it into the creek. It was never found.

Out of respect for her, the French soldiers garrisoned at the small fort eventually arranged for Sister Marie's remains to be shipped to France so she could be buried beside other members of her family. But it's said that, without her head, she could never find peace there, and that her spirit has stayed behind in Acadia to search for it. Her gruesome decapitated apparition has been frightening people around French Fort Cove, especially would-be treasure hunters, for more than two hundred years. As long as she guards the hiding place, it's unlikely that the secret stash of valuables belonging to the French Fort settlers will ever be found.

THE HEADLESS SEA CAPTAIN

St. John's, Newfoundland and Labrador

The year was 1745. The place was St. John's, Newfoundland. The location was a house that a beautiful young woman had called home some years before a man named Samuel Pettyham started renting it. Add betrayal and jealousy, and the stage is set for a tale of terror recorded more than 250 years ago, and passed down from generation to generation ever since.

Pettyham hadn't been living in the house long before he started feeling a little uncomfortable there. What spooked him most was the way the latches on the front and back doors kept lifting mysteriously at night. When he'd fling open the doors to see who was trying to get in, there'd be no one outside. Pettyham found the latch-lifting disturbing, but not enough to make him want to move. Instead, he just made sure every evening that both doors were bolted as well as latched. But one night something happened that nearly scared him to death.

He was coming home from a friend's place when he noticed a strange glow ahead. As he got closer, he saw what looked like the silhouette of a person standing at the end of the street near his front door. Could this be the culprit who'd been trying to get into his house? Pettyham took a few more steps, then froze, petrified. Now he could see that the tall figure before him was a man with no head.

Pettyham bolted back up the street and around the first corner. Trembling, he pounded on the door of a nearby rooming house and begged to be let in. The owner did let him in, and managed to calm him down enough to find out what had happened. Only then did Pettyham learn of the beautiful woman who used to live in his house, and of the two men who had loved her. One had been a neighbour, the other a tall, handsome English sea captain who would visit her whenever he docked his ship in St. John's harbour.

Eventually the neighbour had found out about the captain's late night visits to the woman he thought was his sweetheart. One evening when the captain's ship was in port, he went to his girlfriend's house and, seething with jealousy and rage, he waited in the shadows watching the front door. The moment the captain stepped out of the house into the moonlight, the stalker rushed forward, wielding a razor-sharp sword. One furious swing was all it took. Seconds later, the captain lay dead in street, his bloody head close by.

According to the owner of the boarding house, Pettyham had just seen the sea captain's ghost. Others in the neighbourhood had seen it before, and still others would see it again. The murderer was never caught, so perhaps the captain's spirit kept returning to the scene of the crime to find him.

Whatever the reason, that night in 1745 Samuel Pettyham had no intention of returning home to the spectre of the headless captain, and going to bed. He rented a room where he was and spent the rest of the worst night of his life there.

SPELLBINDER

Montreal, Quebec

Francois-Charles Havard de Beaufort, a soldier from France stationed in Montreal, was always on the lookout for ways to make some extra money. For a small fee, he would impress folks with his card tricks and his knife-handling skills. He had also built a reputation as a sorcerer able to cast magic spells — a practice that Catholic bishops and priests in New France associated with witchcraft and saw as the work of the devil. But one fateful night in 1742, Havard de Beaufort's magic powers appeared to abandon him.

A Montreal shoemaker named Charles Robidoux had been robbed of 300 livres (worth several thousand dollars these days), and the thief was still at large. Could it have been someone he knew? Desperate to recover his money,

Robidoux turned to the young soldier for help. For a fee, Havard de Beaufort said he would expose the thief's identity by casting a spell to make the culprit's face appear in a mirror.

On June 28, 1742, the sorcerer showed up at Robidoux's house. He asked for a table, on which he placed candles, a Catholic prayer book, olive oil, gunpowder and a mirror. Over the next hour or so, he read passages from the prayer book in Latin, burned bits of paper in the candle flames and smeared oil and powder on the mirror in an attempt to conjure up the face of the culprit.

The pops, flames and incantations awed everyone present, but they didn't produce a vision of the thief. In a last-ditch effort to expose the criminal, perhaps among those gathered in Robidoux's parlour, Havard de Beaufort picked up a nearby crucifix, dabbed it with oil, exposed it to the flames and read more sacred prayers aloud. Nothing. Try as he might, he could weave no terrifying magic spell that night.

But the punishment he received for the methods he used was pretty horrific.

The next day when someone reported what he had done, Havard de Beaufort was arrested and tossed into jail, charged with profaning (or disgracefully insulting) the words of the Holy Scripture and with inappropriate and evil use of a holy object — the crucifix.

In August, after a long trial, Havard de Beaufort was found guilty of these crimes. He was banished from New France and sentenced to three years of slave labour in the galleys of the ships belonging to the king of France.

But before he was forced aboard to begin serving his sentence, he had to appear in front of the parish church of Montreal in nothing but a long shirt, carrying a heavy, lighted candle, and wearing a sign that read, "Profaner of holy things." Then he was tied to a wooden frame, dragged from one city crossroad to another and whipped in front of jeering crowds.

An evening of sorcery had had terrifying consequences — ones that Havard de Beaufort could never have imagined. Powerless to save himself, even with magic, he was deported back to France in the autumn of 1742, and was never heard from again.

THE GREY MAN

Montreal, Quebec

Fifty-five years had passed since Toronto children's author Sarah Hartt first saw The Grey Man, but she still remembered it like yesterday.

She and her family — parents, three older brothers and an older sister — were living in a ground-floor apartment in a house on Montreal's Rue St. Urbain back then, in the 1940s.

Sarah was seven at the time, and she and her mother were the only ones at home. She was stretched out on the floor in her brother's bedroom contentedly colouring a picture of a flag when a soft "Oh, no!" from the kitchen made her pause. She figured her mother had probably just dropped something, so she wasn't worried, but she did look away from her picture and toward the open bedroom door.

That's when she saw him — a man wearing a suit

and a hat — walking slowly past the doorway down the hall toward the dining room. He didn't look familiar, his footsteps were silent, and his overall shape appeared greyish and almost translucent. In 2004 Hartt would recall how her seven-year-old self had thought he seemed "see-through-ish." Not sure of what she had just seen, and not wanting to upset her mom, she kept the spooky appearance of The Grey Man to herself.

The second time Sarah saw him, her family had just returned home from a day trip in her father's old Ford. It was a warm summer evening and a gentle rain was falling. As her dad pulled up in front of the house, he suddenly announced that everyone had to stay in the car.

Hartt recalled spending a long time in the hot and crowded Ford that night before her father finally let them get out. She also clearly remembered looking out a rain-spattered window and seeing The Grey Man standing at the front door of her house. Again, Sarah said nothing about seeing him, and her father said nothing about why he kept his family in the car.

Another time, though, when something very spooky happened in the house, Sarah's dad did speak about it. The family was gathered around the dining room table for the evening Passover meal, or seder, when a knife suddenly rose up from the table and dropped back down on a special food-laden plate, cracking it in half. In a fear-filled voice, Sarah's father uttered one unforgettable sentence, "Satan is in this house!" Then he insisted that the ceremonial meal continue as if nothing had happened.

Looking back on that night as an adult, Hartt wondered if some otherworldly presence had been in the house for a long time, and that that was why the landlord had kept the rent so low.

A few years after the seder supper incident, Sarah and one of her brothers were talking about an article in the weekend newspaper about ghosts and hauntings. A sidebar to the article mentioned that ghosts occasionally appeared as "rectangular illuminations."

"I saw that," Sarah blurted out, and told her brother about how she had woken up one night to see a rectangle of light on the wall. Curious, she got out of bed, climbed up on the dresser, and held her hand in front of the bright shape to see if her hand cast a shadow. If it did, she remembered thinking, she would know that the light was bouncing off a mirror or getting in past the window blind in some strange way. But her hand cast no shadow. The light seemed to be coming from the wall itself. Sarah scrambled down from the dresser and headed to her parents' bedroom. When she told her mother what she had seen, her mom said she must have been dreaming and let her snuggle in beside her for the rest of the night.

After Sarah told her brother about the ghostly light, she found the courage to mention The Grey Man. To her amazement, he admitted that he had seen him too. Then he told her about a frightening experience he'd had after coming home from school one afternoon. He had just opened the door when he felt a cold hand clamp its clammy fingers around his wrist. He wrenched his hand away, slammed the door behind him, and ran all the way to their grandmother's house six blocks away.

Buoyed by the knowledge that they had both encountered The Grey Man, the siblings finally decided to tell their mother about him. She was shocked to learn that they had seen him, confessing that he had often appeared in the kitchen, but that she hadn't wanted to frighten anyone by talking about him.

In 1954, when Sarah was twelve, her family moved out of the house on Rue St. Urbain. On moving day, just before the truck loaded with their possessions was about to leave, Sarah and the brother who had been gripped by the ghostly hand were taking one last look around to make sure they had left nothing behind. As they were leaving one room, her brother reached for the light switch on the wall, but he never got to flip it off. Suddenly, the light went out on its own. Maybe, Hartt remembered thinking at the time, this was The Grey Man's way of saying goodbye.

GHOST SAILORS OF THE CHARLES HASKELL

Grand Banks, Newfoundland and Labrador

Seventeen-year-old George W. Scott was one of three Nova Scotians aboard the American-built schooner *Charles Haskell* when it sailed for the cod-rich Grand Banks in March 1866. The rest of the crew was from Gloucester, Massachusetts. On March 6, with a fierce storm brewing, the *Haskell*'s captain decided to make for Georges Bank, at the southwest end of the Grand Banks off Newfoundland and Labrador. There the water would be shallow enough to drop anchor and ride out the storm.

Dozens of other schooner captains had made the same decision, and by midnight most of the north Atlantic fishing fleet in the area was anchored on Georges. But as wave after monstrous wave battered the ships, one broke free of its anchor and, with the wind as its pilot, sailed right toward the *Charles Haskell*. In a desperate attempt to avoid a collision, the *Haskell's* captain gave the order to cut the anchor rope. With barely a minute to spare, his ship drifted out of harm's way, but it too was now out of control and heading straight at another anchored schooner, the *Andrew Jackson*. In every other instance of two ships ramming each other in such a storm, both had been doomed. But in the early hours of March 7, 1866, when these two schooners collided, the *Andrew Jackson* sank with all hands on board and the *Charles Haskell* stayed afloat, with its crew members left horrified but uninjured.

The damaged *Haskell* eventually made it safely back to port for repairs, but young Scott and the rest of the crew refused to sail on her again. There had been rumours she was cursed even before her maiden voyage. Apparently a member of the shipbuilding team who was working on her just before she was launched fell and broke his neck. Local sailors saw his death as a bad omen, a sign of a troubled future. So, after the sinking of the *Andrew Jackson*, the owner of the *Charles Haskell* had an even harder time finding a captain and crew for her.

A few months later, though, the schooner was back at sea fishing for cod. One night, while sailing over Georges Bank with no other ships nearby, two hands on deck got the fright of their lives. As they stared in horror, several oilskin-clad men climbed up over the side. They were dripping wet and their faces looked grey in the moonlight. Without a word, they started moving around as if they were casting fishing nets into the sea. The two horrified men called out to their mates below, and when the rest of the crew stumbled up on deck, they too saw the ghostly crew at work. After a few minutes, as mysteriously as they had appeared, the phantoms slipped back over the rail and into the icy Atlantic waters below.

There's an old superstition that someone who drowns at sea will come back to the ship he was on — if it ever returns to the place where he died. The doomed crew of the *Andrew Jackson* could never return to their ship. The sea had swallowed it up. But when the ship that had sent them to their watery graves sailed over the spot where they had drowned, they boarded it instead. That, according to the crew of the *Charles Haskell*, was the only possible explanation for the nightmarish scene that had unfolded before them as they drifted over Georges Bank.

When his men calmed down enough to set the sails, the *Haskell*'s captain ordered them to change course and make for home. Safe in port, they shared their terrifying story with anyone who would listen. Over the next hundred or so years it would be immortalized in poems and songs, the first most likely being a ballad that appeared in 1874. A poem by Harry L. Marcy called "The Ghostly Crew" was included in *Fishermen's Ballads and Songs of the Sea,* published by Procter Brothers of Gloucester, Massachusetts. Its twenty verses are written in the first person, as if a *Haskell* crew member were telling the tale. The eighth stanza refers to the earlier accident:

...

> *The trip before, our schooner,*
> *She was on Georges then,*
> *Ran down another vessel*
> *And sunk her and her men.*

Two stanzas later, the sailor narrator begins to describe how the horrifying scene unfolded:

For in the dim dark watches
I felt a chilly dread
Come on me, just as if I heard
One calling from the dead.

And o'er our rail there clambered
All silent, one by one,
A dozen dripping sailors —
Just wait till I am done.

...

Right on to deck they clambered
And not a voice we heard,
They moved about before us
And never spoke a word.

Their faces pale and sea wet
Shown ghastly through the night,
Each took his place as fairly
As if he had a right.

After describing how the sea-drenched fishermen went about their work, the poem sums up what the *Charles Haskell*'s crew must have felt that fateful night:

...

But 'twas the same poor fellows
I think, God rest their souls,
That our old craft ran under
That time on Georges shoals.

And there you have my story,
And 'twas just as I say,
And I've believed in spirits
Since that time anyway.

After that night on board the cursed schooner with the phantom crew, the *Haskell's* men certainly must have shared the feelings of the poem's narrator. Even if they hadn't believed in spirits before that trip, they did afterwards. And they believed that the ghosts were the spirits of the drowned seamen from the *Andrew Jackson.*

A MOTHER'S NIGHTMARE

Trinity Bay, Newfoundland and Labrador

Over the centuries, powerful north Atlantic storms have claimed the lives of many brave, hardworking Maritimers.

No one was more aware of this than Mary Crewe, who lived in a small outport community on Trinity Bay, in Newfoundland. She had nearly lost her husband, Reuben, in 1911 when the sealing ship he was on sank in the Gulf of St. Lawrence. Sealing was dangerous work that involved leaving the safety of a ship to go out on the ice and hunt the animals that were such an important source of food, skins and oil — and of wages that were needed to buy other supplies. After his brush with death, Crewe had given up such work, and for that Mary was truly grateful.

But in March 1914, her sixteen-year-old son Albert John announced that he'd been offered a job on the sealing ship *Newfoundland*, and that he really wanted to take it. Not only could Mary not change his mind, but she also had to accept her husband's decision to go with him. She understood how much he wanted to try to protect Albert from the dangers he knew the young man might face.

As she would later tell her daughter, Mary awoke suddenly one night to see her beloved husband and son kneeling beside her bed. Their heads were bowed in prayer and they appeared calm. But seeing them like this started Mary's heart pounding. Reuben and Albert John weren't home that night. They were out among the ice floes, working off the *Newfoundland*. Or so she thought.

What happened to the *Newfoundland*'s sealers after the wooden ship became trapped in the ice on March 30, 1914, is recorded in the reports of three hearings held to investigate the tragedy. The icy grip closing in on the ship . . . the sealers being sent off it to walk twelve to fifteen kilometres to another ship, the *Stephano*, that had reported seeing seals . . . the blinding blizzard . . . the confusion and miscommunication . . . these and many other horrific details are included in those reports. So are the names of the seventy-eight men who either drowned or froze to death during the most tragic sealing disaster in Newfoundland and Labrador's history.

Reuben and Albert John's names are on that list. Their frozen bodies were found on the ice. They were holding on to each other, as if to keep warm, and there was a look of calm on their faces.

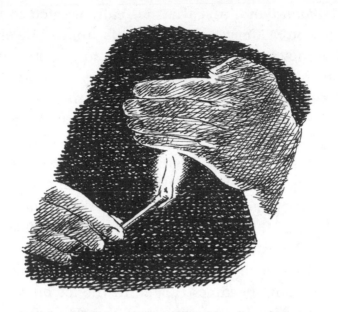

THE SCREAMING TUNNEL

Niagara Falls, Ontario

The tunnel running under the railway tracks off Warner Road in Niagara Falls, Ontario, is such a spooky place that Canadian filmmaker David Cronenberg used it as the backdrop for a gruesome murder in his 1983 film, *The Dead Zone*, based on a book with the same name by the master of the horror story, author Stephen King. But there seems to be no way of verifying which one of the scary stories associated with the tunnel has made it such a spooky place.

One version of the tunnel's tale of terror dates back more than a century. It involves a girl trapped inside a nearby house where a fire broke out. The girl finally managed to escape the blazing inferno. Crazed with pain, she ran from the inferno into the tunnel with her clothes ablaze, and collapsed and died there. Another version has a girl being set on fire there after her father learned that his wife had won custody of their daughter following a bitter divorce battle. And still another version has a young girl being assaulted and murdered in the tunnel.

There are no records of such tragedies or hideous crimes taking place in the tunnel, but the stories about why it's haunted remain to this day and, over the years, many local young people have dared to check out if it really is. Late at night they slowly enter the tunnel and light a match. When the match goes out, they're supposed to hear the screams of a young girl. Those who do usually run screaming from the tunnel themselves. Those who don't, heave a sigh of relief.

The Screaming Tunnel in Niagara Falls, Ontario

FEAR AROUND THE CAMPFIRE

Dunnville, Ontario

The tale of Anson Minor is probably an urban myth — a story people claim to be true because it happened, or so they say, to someone they knew or to someone who knew someone who knew . . .

The terror associated with the story rests not in its truth, but with the experiences of young campers who have believed in it over the years and been scared out of their wits by it.

A popular version of Minor's tale says he lived in Dunnville, Ontario, on the shores of Lake Erie. In the 1920s he lost his leg in a tractor accident on his farm. He was fitted with a wooden leg, but he hated it, and coping with the loss of a limb slowly drove him mad. He finally took his overpowering frustration out on his family, murdering his wife and son. It's said he died several years later in a hospital for the criminally insane.

After Minor died, his heirs sold the property, and in the 1940s new owners turned it into a summer camp called Camp Kvutzah — unaware at first of the rumours that Minor's ghost wasn't in any rush to leave his old homestead. Over the years, a few campers did see a wispy shape in the woods, so the belief that Minor was haunting the camp grew stronger, especially when camp counsellors used that notion to persuade new campers to hurry up and get inside at bedtime. To make their point more effectively, a few counsellors embellished the story a bit, adding the well-known "fact" that Minor really hated campers staying on his land, and that he had a ball and chain attached to the ankle of his real, not wooden, leg. With that detail added to the Minor tale, the occasional sound of a chain rattling could send even the least co-operative youngster scurrying indoors.

The last summer before Camp Kvutzah closed for good, one young counsellor decided to try and impress another counsellor he really liked. He bragged about not being afraid of Minor's ghost, adding that he didn't even believe it existed. Then he agreed to be tied up to a tree deep in the woods and spend the night there. The next morning when the other counsellors went to untie him, they found that his hair had turned completely white and he had a glazed look in his eyes. When his friends ask him what had happened, he wouldn't talk about it — not then, and not ever again. Everyone assumed that Minor had paid him a visit.

It's said that after Camp Kvutzah closed, Minor's ghost finally moved on — but not to some peaceful afterlife. He just moved on to another summer camp, and another and another, haunting campers all across the province, especially on July 1, the anniversary of his death. The sound of him stomping around in the bush on his wooden leg, dragging a ball and chain, warns them that he's near. At least that's what some camp counsellors tell youngsters when they arrive on the Canada Day weekend, looking forward to their first stay at a summer camp.

After hearing Minor's story, the campers huddle in their sleeping bags and lie awake in the darkness, hoping they won't hear any strange sounds outside their tent or bunkhouse. There's terror in their hearts, even if the tale of Anson Minor isn't really true.

GHOSTS ON HIS MIND

Canmore, Alberta

In 1994 Don Hill — musician, filmmaker, writer and CBC Radio host — was a haunted man.

He was haunted by what he and his family had experienced while living in a house they had bought in Canmore, Alberta. The unexplained noises, the chilling sense of an invisible presence, the sudden overwhelming waves of fear, and the ghostly apparition of a glowing life-sized shape — it was finally, in 1994, all too much for Hill and his family. He put the house up for sale, and they moved out as soon as it was sold.

But Hill wasn't able to hit a mental delete button and get rid of the memories of the terrifying experiences. So he decided to try to find out why they had occurred. Over the next four years Hill interviewed doctors, scientists and spiritual advisors in search of answers.

One of the people he consulted was Dr. Michael Persinger, a professor of neuroscience — the study of the brain and how it works — at Laurentian University in Sudbury, Ontario. After talking with Persinger by phone, Hill went to Sudbury to learn more about his work and to take part in one of the professor's experiments.

In Persinger's brain-science lab — a small, soundproof chamber lit only by a single red light — Hill sat in a chair, eyes covered, with a tight-fitting, electrically wired helmet on his head. Then he let his brain be stimulated by electromagnetic waves coming from a controlled flow of electricity through the wires in the helmet.

Imagine his surprise and horror when, after several minutes, he "saw" an apparition that looked a lot like the ghost that had haunted his house in Canmore. But had the ghost followed him, or was it simply the product of unusual electrical activity in his brain? After years of research, Persinger thought that the second explanation was a possible answer to Hill's question. According to the neuroscientist's theory, electrical activity in the brain may also account for people's beliefs that they've seen aliens or angels.

But if electromagnetic waves explain the reappearance of the ghost that haunted Hill's house in Canmore, what caused the unusual electrical brain activity in the first place? And not just in Hill's head, but in the heads of the rest of his family? These are questions to which Hill never got an answer . . .

HAUNTED ROOMS FOR RENT

Toronto, Ontario

One chilly January day in 1886, a widow and her daughter moved their possessions into their new home. They were looking forward to living in the roomy upper-floor flat they had just rented in an old house on Gerrard Street in Toronto. The next morning they were moving their things out of the house as fast as they could carry them. Their first night there had been absolutely terrifying.

The first thing they noticed was how cold the place was, even though they had managed to get a good fire going in the fireplace. Tired, they snuggled under extra bedclothes and eventually fell asleep. But not for long. Just before midnight they were awakened by loud banging and slamming sounds downstairs. And then, even though their bedroom door was shut, a blast of wintry air blew through the room, lifting the blankets right off their bed. The mother went out into the hall and called downstairs to Mr. Farrel, the owner who lived on the lower floor, asking him to shut the doors. But he had no idea what she was talking about.

Worried that her imagination was playing tricks on her, the mother went back to bed, calmed her daughter down, and said they should try to get some more sleep. But sleep never came. A while later, a dark mysterious shape drifted over the bed, leaving them trembling with fear, as did the thumping footsteps they heard moving along the hall.

Mother and daughter clung to each other until dawn. Then they rose, got dressed, packed their bags and left, telling Mr. Farrel that nothing could make them stay another minute in the upstairs flat they had hoped to call home.

DREAM WARNING

Tagish Lake, Yukon

Tagish Lake is a long, narrow lake crossing the border between the Yukon and British Columbia. For hundreds of years, members of the Gwich'in Nation lived a nomadic life along its shores. Then gold was discovered at Bonanza Creek in 1896, and the Klondike Gold Rush began. Prospectors from the south started moving into and through the area. Today the Klondike Highway follows the western arm of the lake in the Yukon much as the prospectors did more than a century ago.

Although the lake is rather isolated, it made news around the world after a large meteorite crashed into its frozen surface in January of 2000. A local resident, Jim Brook, collected the 200-gram meteorite and other smaller pieces of space rock, and made them available to researchers. They were very excited by his find. The Tagish meteorite turned out to be the most pristine, or uncontaminated, meteorite they had ever analyzed — and it was the very first one they identified as having come all the way from a band of asteroids between Mars and Jupiter.

The lake had also caught the interest of UFO (Unidentified Flying Object) researchers. In the early 1970s three people — two men and a woman — reported seeing seven large, round objects moving slowly in the sky over the lake. One of the men took a picture of the mysterious, bright orbs, and the other sent the photo to weather officials in Ottawa in the hope of learning what the UFOs were. He was eventually told that any information about them was classified.

But the most unusual event reported about the lake made the news back in 1916, when a somewhat strange article appeared in the *The Nome Daily Nugget,* the daily newspaper at the time in Nome, Alaska. The article recounted how Don Mack, a mining engineer working in northern Canada and Alaska, had written to a woman named Ethel Williams to thank her for saving him from drowning in Tagish Lake.

In his letter, Mack explained that he had been crossing the frozen lake by sled with three Indigenous men and a French Canadian when they decided to camp for the night on a small island. During the night Mack had a vivid dream in which a young woman appeared. She identified herself as Ethel Williams of Syracuse, New York, and she warned him not to travel in the direction he planned to go the next day — because the snow-covered ice there was dangerously thin. When Mack awoke, the other men were packing up and getting ready to set off again, so he told

Tagish Lake in winter

them about his disturbing dream and suggested they follow a new route. But they just laughed at him and set off as planned, leaving him to continue on his journey alone.

Mack wrote that he had detoured around the dangerous area he had been warned about by the apparition and made it safely to Skagway, but the four other men never showed up. Worried, he organized a search party to go back and look for them. Several days later, he was both saddened and stunned when he found the missing men's canoes and some of their gear floating in the lake's icy waters — very close to the place he had been warned to avoid. Mack and the other searchers presumed the four had drowned. Their bodies were never found.

Back in his office in Juneau, Alaska, Mack couldn't get thoughts of his dream and his narrow escape out of his head. After doing some research, he learned that a young woman named Ethel Williams did indeed live in Syracuse, New York, and he couldn't resist writing to her. He wanted to thank her for saving his life. Someone in Ethel's family — perhaps Ethel herself — was so amazed when the letter arrived that it was reported to a local newspaper, and the article that appeared was eventually picked up by *The Nome Daily Nugget.*

Ethel had been astonished when she read the letter because she had never heard of Don Mack, or Tagish Lake, and she had absolutely no way of knowing the ice conditions there in the late fall. But apparently Mack had met her once — in a dream he would never forget.

NiGHT ViSiON

North Atlantic Ocean

In the 1930s Joseph Boyd, a sea captain from Yarmouth, Nova Scotia, told folklorist Helen Creighton about a dream that *he* would never forget.

He had been serving as his brother's first mate on a sailing ship bound for New York in the late 1890s when his brother told him about a frightening dream he had just had. In it, several sailors were tied to the rigging of a badly damaged, wave-swept ship, their hands outstretched as if pleading for help.

Joe kept thinking about the dream as he went about the stormy morning's tasks. Finally, for no good reason he could think of, he made the tricky climb up the rigging and scanned the churning waves. To his amazement, off in the distance he spotted a foundering vessel with all but one mast gone, and with men with outstretched arms tied to the rigging.

Joe shouted out the order to change course and, after hours of hazardous manoeuvering, the crew of his ship managed to rescue sixteen sailors perilously close to death. And Joe was convinced they would have died if it hadn't been for his brother's dream.

Sadly, some members of the shipwrecked crew had been washed overboard when the storm's fury first hit. Perhaps the dream was a last desperate effort by the ghost of one of those drowned men to save his fellow sailors before he journeyed into eternity.

A DEADLY DRIVE

Fredericton, New Brunswick

The brutal murder of taxi driver Norman Phillip Burgoyne in January of 1949 sent shockwaves of horror through Fredericton, New Brunswick.

Just thirty-four years old when he was killed, Burgoyne was married and the father of three young children. His wife reported him missing when he didn't return home after answering a Friday night call for a taxi from the Canadian Legion Hall. Three days later his body was found stuffed into the trunk of his cab at the southeastern outskirts of the city, on Wilsey Road.

Burgoyne's killers had badly botched their efforts to conceal their crime, leaving behind plenty of clues to their identities, and it took police just a couple of days to find them. Rufus Hamilton, aged twenty-two, and his brother

George, twenty-three, were charged with the murder. During their trial, George told the court how Rufus had bludgeoned Burgoyne with a hammer. Then they had robbed him. The Hamiltons were found guilty and sentenced to death by hanging. Both sentences were carried out on the same day in July of 1949.

There are those who believe that the two young men, united by their deaths just minutes apart, remained together in the afterlife — and that their ghosts still haunt Fredericton. The Hammer Brothers, as they came to be known, have been reported wandering through some of the city's back alleys. They've also been seen thumbing a ride into town, but no one will stop to pick them up — especially not along Wilsey Road.

THE GHOSTLY GALLEY

Placentia Bay, Newfoundland

About 2800 years ago the Greeks and Phoenicians started building galleys — large ships propelled by oars — that were fast enough and strong enough to ram and sink enemy vessels. These warships had one, two or three rows of oars, powered by fifty, one hundred or one hundred and seventy men. With the oarsmen rowing steadily, galleys could maintain average speeds of about ten to fifteen kilometres an hour. Yet, no matter how well they rowed, even with the help of a single sail, they would not have set out to cross a large ocean like the Atlantic. They would have perished long before they reached the shores of Newfoundland.

But in the 1920s, centuries after these ships had

disappeared into history, a galley suddenly appeared in Placentia Bay, Newfoundland, to the west of the Avalon Peninsula. It was complete with a ghostly crew working two rows of oars. More terrifying still, the ship was on fire. People on shore spoke of how they could feel the fire's heat and hear the unbearable cries of the men aboard as flames engulfed the galley. And yet the ship sailed on until it suddenly vanished.

Back then, dozens of folks living in fishing communities around the bay reported sightings of the horrifying apparition. However, it has now been more than eighty years since anyone has seen the blazing vision and heard the mournful cries of the ghostly oarsmen who travelled so far off course in place and time.

A GHOST ASKS WHY

Muskoka, Ontario

Jean Kozocari first saw a ghost in the 1930s. She was a young child at the time, spending the summer at her grandparents' riverside lodge in the Muskokas, Ontario's popular cottage country.

Two guests who had just arrived at the lodge were newlyweds. Competitive swimmers, they were honeymooning in the area so they could continue training for upcoming national trials. The day they decided to go for a swim was like so many others that summer — warm and sunny, with just a gentle breeze drifting through the trees. Other guests had warned the couple of a dangerous undertow in a turbulent section of the river, but they didn't seem concerned. They strolled down the path hand in hand, waded into the water until it was deep enough, and swam away.

Jean was playing outside then. She was still outside some time later — when the husband clambered back up the path gasping for breath and begging for help. People were shouting and running toward him. Jean was frightened. She was also confused. She could see guests rushing to put boats in the water when the frantic husband told them how his bride had disappeared in a swirling eddy and his desperate search to find her had failed. But Jean didn't understand — because she could also see his wife.

The young woman was standing near her husband. She was dripping wet, bent over slightly, and sobbing. And in the midst of all the noise and confusion, Jean could hear her moaning again and again, "How *could* you?" But people were still heading for the river to look for her and, gradually, it dawned on Jean that no one else could see her.

As dusk fell, the search was called off, and guests slowly returned to the lodge, talking in hushed tones about the missing bride. Her body was never found, but Jean saw her several times over the next few weeks, standing on a small island in the river, wet hair plastered around her face and doubled over as if in pain. And each time Jean saw her, she heard her cry out, "Why did he do it? I loved him."

Jean was too young at the time to make sense of what she saw that summer, but nearly fifty years later she would recall details of what had happened in *A Gathering of Ghosts*, a book she co-authored with Robin Skelton in which she described several other times she has seen, heard or sensed ghostly presences. The drowned bride was the first of many ghosts she would encounter over her lifetime, but memories of her often haunted Jean. Had the young woman's death been just a tragic accident? Or something much more sinister — a murder? Jean could never forget hearing her plead, "How *could* you?" that summer so long ago — nor stop imagining what she could have meant.

DEAD RED EYES

Clarke's Beach, Newfoundland and Labrador

Drowning claimed the life of another young woman whose spirit appears to have lingered after death. At least that's the explanation given for the terror three girls experienced at Clarke's Beach on the island of Newfoundland in the 1980s.

At the mouth of the North River, Clarke's Beach is one of several picturesque towns dotting the southwest coast of Conception Bay. The train no longer runs past the town, but part of the old railway bridge crossing the river is still there. That's where the teenagers were heading when they went for a walk one summer evening. It's also where they had the scare of their lives.

As they approached the span, the girls noticed a dark shape perched on it. Getting closer, they saw that it was a young woman in a bathing suit drying herself with a towel. She didn't seem to hear them coming. Wondering who she was, they took a few more steps toward her. Suddenly she turned and looked straight at them — and they froze in fright. Her eyes were glowing red like burning coals. Stumbling backward, the girls ran screaming from the bridge.

Several residents weren't too surprised when they heard about the spine-chilling apparition that had left the three teenagers so shaken. According to them, the girls hadn't been the first to report seeing the disturbing vision of the spooky female, and they might not be the last to do so, either. Some locals say she is the ghost of a young woman who, many years earlier, had gone to the bridge to meet her lover for a midnight swim. When he didn't show up as planned, she decided to go swimming anyway — alone. That decision proved fatal. But every now and then, she still returns — searching for her lover, probing the darkness with her glowing red eyes.

A FATHER'S FAREWELL

Near Fort Augustus, Northwest Territories

In the early 1800s, competition was fierce among fur trading companies operating in what would become Canada's
prairie provinces and Northwest Territories. The Hudson
Bay Company, the North West Company and the XY
Company were busy building forts throughout the area —
in hopes of attracting Indigenous and Métis trappers eager
to trade their furs.

James King was a trader for the North West Company
operating around the North Saskatchewan River in 1802.
That year his manager, John McDonald, asked him to
go and meet with a group of Indigenous people who had
a large number of furs to sell. King had a reputation for
being a tough man to deal with. Nevertheless, McDonald
warned him to be careful of another rough and ready

character named La Mothe, an XY Company clerk who was apparently going after the same furs.

King set out by sleigh from Fort Augustus, near the current site of Fort Saskatchewan, Alberta, telling his wife that he'd be back in three days. The second night he was gone, his six-year-old daughter woke, crying. When King's wife tried to comfort her, the little girl explained that she'd just seen her father near her in their tent — and that his neck was strangely red. After hearing her mother's reassuring explanation that the frightening vision had just been a bad dream, the girl went back to sleep. A few hours later, though, she was wide awake again, and she was very afraid. Her father, she told her mother, had returned. He had stood at the foot of the bed, watching her. And his neck was still all red.

The next day, King's wife told several people at the fort about what had happened during the night, and they all agreed with her that bad dreams had caused the girl such distress. They changed their minds, however, when the trading party returned with a sleigh loaded down with furs — and with the bloody body of James King. The night before, he had been in a fight with La Mothe, the XY Company's man. La Mothe had shot him through the neck.

Had James King's spirit returned that fateful night to spend a few final moments with his little daughter?

THE INVISIBLE FRIEND

Nanaimo, British Columbia

It's not unusual for a young child to invent an imaginary playmate. But when several children at a daycare centre in Nanaimo, British Columbia, started chatting with the same make-believe friend, caregivers wondered what was going on. A few youngsters even drew similar pictures of the mysterious child — in a white nightgown, playing with a red ball. Could it be that the children were seeing one of the spirits said to haunt Beban House?

Beban House was built in the late 1920s by Frank Beban, an immigrant from New Zealand who made his fortune in the lumber business. Beban moved into the impressive log mansion with his wife and four children in 1930, and lived there until his death in 1952. In 1953 the city of Nanaimo bought the house and the more than sixty hectares of Beban estate land surrounding it. Over the years the city put the property to good use, creating parkland and playing fields, and building a sports complex and other facilities used by various community groups.

But for four decades the mansion itself was largely neglected — until it was restored in the 1990s. In 1997 it became the new home to Nanaimo's tourism bureau. Before that a daycare centre had occupied the main floor. Some of the children attending the centre then, and several people who have worked in the building, appear to have one thing in common — an unexplained encounter with an eerie presence in the house.

Various organizations have offices in Beban House now, and some of their staff have reported unsettling experiences such as the sounds of dishes clattering in an empty room, water taps turning on mysteriously in a washroom, and cupboard doors and filing cabinet drawers flying open on their own. People have heard light footsteps scurrying up and down the stairs, and heavy footsteps stomping around in an empty room on the second floor. A woman has appeared suddenly in a hallway and then vanished as quickly as she came. And late at night when no one was in the building, passersby have seen a glowing light in the upstairs windows.

Frank Beban and his wife loved their beautiful home. Could it be that they have been reluctant to leave it? Is Frank walking heavy-footed around his den, and is he the one opening the doors to the cupboard where he once kept his finest Scotch whisky? And is his wife appearing in the hall, or clinking cups and saucers as she prepares to serve tea to some of her lady friends? Some people think so. But what about the lighter footsteps and the water taps and lights being turned on? Could another spirit — a young and mischievous one — also be lingering in the mansion?

A few people have felt particularly uneasy in some rooms in the basement where the Beban family's servants had lived. One of these servants, a Chinese boy, had died there, and a psychic researcher who visited the house strongly sensed his spirit's presence on that lower floor. Is it his ghost, with hair in a traditional Chinese braid, that appeared in the daycare children's artwork? Maybe, after so many lonely years in the empty house, the boy's spirit introduced itself to the children, hoping they would want to play with him and his red ball.

HALLOWEEN HORROR

Saint John, New Brunswick

There are those who believe that an unsettling air remains at the scene of a particularly vicious crime long after it is committed. That may explain why, for years after the murders of Maggie Vail and her baby girl, Ella May, horses would balk as they approached a certain spot on Black River Road in Saint John, New Brunswick.

In September of 1869, children out berry-picking discovered the skeletal remains of mother and child in a wooded area near the road. They couldn't be identified right away, but as news of the horrifying discovery spread, people came forward with clues that led authorities to identify the victims and, after two weeks, to charge a man named John A. Munroe with their murders.

The people of Saint John were shocked. John Munroe

was a pillar of the community. He was a well-known architect who had designed several buildings in the town. Though he had a wife and two young children, he had taken up with Maggie Vail — and little Ella May was his daughter. Munroe claimed he was innocent of the murders, but he was tried, found guilty and sentenced to death. The week before he was hanged in February of 1870, he finally confessed that he had killed Maggie and Ella on October 31 — All Hallow's Eve — in 1868.

John A. Munroe is buried in Fernhill Cemetery in Saint John. Over the years a story has persisted that on Halloween night an eerie green glow emanates from beneath his tombstone. It's said that teenagers dare one another to steal onto the property and check it out, but no one has spoken publicly about doing so. Were they too afraid to go? Or too afraid of what they saw? Whatever their reasons, they remain as silent as the grave.

The gravestone of John A. Munroe

BLOOD IN THE BARBERSHOP

Barkerville, British Columbia

A ghostly apparition played a part in another infamous case of murder — the fatal shooting of Charles Morgan Blessing in northern British Columbia in 1866.

Blessing, like so many other prospectors, was following the gold that had been luring thousands of people to the Pacific coast ever since the rush to California began in 1848. Blessing had left San Francisco for B.C.'s Cariboo Mountains in 1866, hoping for another chance to make his fortune. He was heading for Barkerville, a boom town that sprang up after Billy Barker struck it rich mining gold on nearby Williams Creek in 1862.

Along the way, Blessing met a travelling barber named Wellington Delaney Moses, and the two men journeyed on together. Later they were joined by a third man, James

Barry, whom Moses thought was a bit of a suspicious character. When the trio reached Quesnel, Moses decided to stay for a while. He could earn a little extra money there giving haircuts to men who stopped over in the town to pick up supplies. Since he and Blessing had become friends, he promised to look him up when he reached Barkerville.

When Moses finally arrived in Barkerville, he opened his own barbershop. Business was brisk, and Moses figured his new friend Blessing would have no trouble finding him in town. But he never arrived. After several weeks, though, James Barry did — alone. He told Moses that Blessing had hurt his foot and had decided he couldn't make it to Barkerville.

A view of Barkerville, 1868

Moses had a gut feeling Barry wasn't telling the truth. He became even more concerned about what had happened when a customer showed up at the shop wearing a gold nugget lapel pin. The nugget, shaped like a skull, was unusual, but Moses had seen one just like it a few months earlier — pinned to the jacket of Charles Blessing. Questioned by Moses about how he had got the pin, the customer said a dance hall girl in town had given it to him. Moses found the woman and learned that James Barry had given it to her soon after he had shown up in Barkerville.

This news fuelled Moses' suspicions about Blessing's fate, but not nearly as much as did a horrifying incident a few weeks later. The barber was in his shop waiting for customers when Blessing suddenly appeared, wanting a shave. His friend was a mess. He was dirty, his clothes were in tatters, and the gleam of life had gone from his eyes. Moses immediately prepared a hot towel and wrapped Blessing's face in it, then reached for his razor. When he turned back, he recoiled in horror. The towel covering Blessing's face was wet through with blood. Trembling, he reached for a corner of the cloth, but suddenly the chair was empty. Blessing was gone, and so were any doubts Moses might have had that something terrible had happened to him.

Moses travelled to nearby Richmond to tell a judge about his suspicions and, based on his evidence about the gold pin and the discovery of Blessing's body hidden in the bush along the trail, the judge ordered Barry arrested. Blessing had been shot in the head — and Barry owned a gun that could have caused that fatal wound, adding to the case that was built against him when he was tried for Blessing's murder. Judge Matthew Begbie, perhaps

British Columbia's most famous judge, heard the case, and in August of 1867, found Barry guilty and sentenced him to hang. Barry's trip to the gallows was the first public execution in the Cariboo district of British Columbia.

After Blessing's corpse was discovered, Moses arranged for its burial and, with the help of donations from his customers, paid for a headstone for the grave. But it was only when Barry was convicted that Moses finally felt he had done all he could to get justice for the man he had befriended along the gold rush trail. Surely now Blessing would truly rest in peace, and the terrifying spectre of his tormented spirit would never haunt Moses again.

Chief Justice Sir Matthew Begbie, ca. 1875

Spirits Past and Present

The ghosts of Barkerville's colourful past still walk the streets here, as living locals dressed in period costumes recreate the gold-rush era for visitors. The famed Judge Begbie holds court, miners dig for gold, a blacksmith works his forge, and a long-skirted schoolmarm greets rambunctious pupils. It's all in good fun, and it definitely makes history come alive for tourists.

But there are a few characters who appear in Barkerville who were never given parts in the re-enactment scripts. And if they ever lived in the town, they're not alive now. There's the mysterious fellow sporting a top hat and tails who suddenly appears briefly on the left side of the stage at the Theatre Royal. There's also the attractive blond woman wearing a white dress who has been known to startle male guests by materializing in their rooms at the St. George Hotel. And often, when everyone has gone home for the night at the museum housed in the former Barkerville Hotel, people have reported seeing a ghostly apparition of a woman looking out of a window upstairs.

No one seems to know who these restless spirits might be, but their presence adds new meaning to the "ghost town" label that's often given to settlements in the area that were abandoned when the gold ran out.

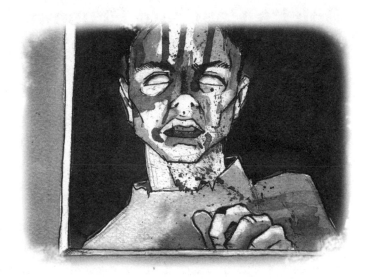

GHOSTLY BUSINESS

Halifax, Nova Scotia

In 1820 Alexander Keith, a young immigrant from Scotland, bought a brewery in Halifax and began a tradition of brewing fine beers in Nova Scotia. He had learned the business from an uncle in England a few years earlier, and used what he had learned to become a very successful businessman. He also became a prominent politician, actively involved in the development of Halifax and in the move to have Nova Scotia join Canada's Confederation in 1867. But he never stopped taking pride in his reputation as an excellent brewer.

Even now, he seems to linger, checking on the high standards he set nearly two centuries ago. Several workers at the Brewery Market on Halifax's Lower Water Street, home to Alexander Keith's Nova Scotia Brewery, are convinced it's his ghost that haunts the place. They've been startled when it makes its presence known in different parts of the establishment, but they're not too frightened by the sound of footsteps wandering through empty halls. They figure it's just Keith keeping an eye on what they're doing in his name.

However, there are a few very disturbing reports of *another* phantom lurking around the Brewery Market, and this one isn't friendly. It's the gory reflection of a blood-covered man that suddenly appears in a washroom mirror. When a terrified customer turns around to see what horror is behind him, he finds there's nothing there — and a hasty dash for the exit seems the best thing to do.

CREEPY CONFINEMENT

Ottawa, Ontario

Visitors looking for an inexpensive place to stay while touring Canada's capital often check into Ottawa's main youth hostel and, for some, the stay there is truly unforgettable.

The hostel is located at 75 Nicholas Street in a massive stone building that was home to the Carleton County Jail for more than a hundred years — from 1862 to 1972. Officially, only three hangings took place at the jail, but guards sometimes took it upon themselves to string up a prisoner from a beam near the gallows on the eighth floor, then cut down the body and watch it plummet to the courtyard below. Hundreds of other people died because of torturous treatment and miserable conditions in the jail. And thousands more — men, women and children — died when, as newly arrived immigrants infected with scarlet fever, they were kept in the basement, in an attempt to control the spread of this highly contagious disease. The bodies of the infection-riddled victims were burned and their remains were buried on the grounds of the jail. Not surprising, then, are the many reports suggesting that the Ottawa Jail Hostel has some very creepy residents serving longer-than-life sentences.

The most infamous criminal to be hanged at the jail was Patrick James Whelan. He was convicted of assassinating Thomas D'Arcy McGee, one of Canada's Fathers of Confederation. Whelan maintained his innocence right up to his death — an execution that was watched by a sensation-seeking crowd of five thousand. Since that fateful day in 1868, people have seen him walk toward the gallows many more times. His ghost has appeared in

The courthouse and jail, ca. 1870–1880

his cell on Death Row too, and even in the rooms of a few horrified guests.

Hostel visitors have also had nerve-racking encounters with other spirits that haunt the jail. They've been nudged in the back by an invisible presence, they've been startled by shadowy figures showing up at their doors, and they've been sent shivering from a location that is suddenly engulfed by icy blasts. They've heard chains rattling, pipes banging, cell doors clanging, children crying, women wailing, and men talking in empty rooms and hallways. And they've even had to listen to tales of a legendary evil vampire hiding out in the building — one rumoured to have feasted on the blood of children.

Despite such disturbing reports of otherworldly activity, the hostel continues to attract guests looking for reasonably priced rooms in an unusual setting rich in local history. Some even specifically check in hoping for a supernatural thrill. But folks who are easily frightened might want to think twice about staying there. The emotional price might be far too high for them to pay.

DEADMAN'S ISLAND

Halifax, Nova Scotia

Elegant yachts now moor along the mainland side of Melville Island, a small island near the head of the Northwest Arm of Halifax Harbour in Nova Scotia. But in the early 1800s, this was a much grimmer place.

Back then, British navy warships dropped anchor there to unload French and American prisoners of war captured during the Napoleonic Wars and the War of 1812. The British had built a large military prison there in 1803 specifically to house such prisoners until they could be exchanged for their own captured soldiers and sailors. The captives were warned off trying to escape by being told, untruthfully, that the waters around the island were filled with hungry sharks.

But infectious diseases did claim the lives of some of

the men confined there in such close quarters. Their bodies were wrapped in shrouds and rowed to a nearby spit of land that prisoners called Target Hill — and that came to be known as Deadman's Island. Here the remains of close to two hundred American sailors and soldiers were buried in shallow graves. So were the bodies of one hundred black slaves who had abandoned the American army for the British and then succumbed to smallpox. Then came the Irish immigrants who had died of typhus fever.

Most of the prison buildings on Melville Island burned down in 1936, but over the years people would wander around Deadman's Island looking for relics of its past. And when they did, they occasionally discovered skeletal remains, giving rise to stories of ghosts haunting the old graveyard. Boys would challenge each other to sneak out to the end of the spit at night, and a few brave souls did spend some spine-tingling moments there, coming back with tales of spooky shapes moving around in the dark.

Some of those stories didn't seem so far-fetched, though, when workers became involved in preparations for building a development on Deadman's Island a few years ago. They felt uneasy when unusual lights began to appear among the trees they were planning to cut down. Glowing fires and mysterious lights have also been spotted by people looking across the harbour toward the island, and Alan Hatfield, a psychic visiting the site in 2002, heard the voices of three distinct male spirits.

In the late 1990s some Halifax residents started lobbying to have the spit of land preserved as a historic site, and they were eventually successful. Development plans were halted in 2000 when the city bought the property so it could be respectfully preserved as a burial ground. And in May of 2005, representatives of both the American and

Canadian armed forces took part in a ceremony marking the installation of a bronze plaque on a granite base to honour the memory of the Americans buried there.

At last, it seems, many restless souls have found peace. But strange lights are still occasionally spotted on Deadman's Island. And teenagers are still daring each other to head out that way after dark.

HEADLESS MARY

Montreal, Quebec

Most people don't go looking for ghosts, and most don't want ghosts to come looking for them. But for more than one hundred and thirty years, curiosity-seekers have gathered in Griffintown, an area of downtown Montreal near the Lachine Canal, hoping to see the ghost of a woman looking for her head. And over the years parents living in the area have warned their misbehaving youngsters that the headless ghost would come after them while she wandered around searching for it.

Griffintown was a bustling, working-class neighbourhood of Montreal where thousands of Irish immigrants settled when they arrived in Canada in the nineteenth century. Life was hard for many of the people living there. It was certainly hard for two friends, Mary Gallagher and

Susan Kennedy, who were staying in a flat in a house at the corner of William and Murray Streets in the summer of 1879. On the night of June 27, they'd been socializing with a man named Michael Flanagan when they got into a terrible fight — and Mary Gallagher was killed. According to court documents, Susan Kennedy had knocked her to the floor and whacked her several times with an axe, chopping off her head. A neighbour living downstairs said the blows overhead were so violent that the ceiling plaster cracked, sending pieces showering down.

Susan Kennedy was found guilty of murdering her best friend. Her sentence — death by hanging — was supposed to be carried out on December 5, 1879, but a judge finally spared her life and sent her to prison instead. She was eventually paroled, after serving sixteen years in the Kingston Penitentiary in Ontario.

A Griffintown street during the spring floods, 1873

In the years following Mary Gallagher's death, several people reported seeing her on the streets of Griffintown, dressed as she had always been in life. And even though her ghost didn't always appear headless, people said she was looking for her head. As the number of Mary Gallagher sightings dwindled over time, locals began to talk about how she just appeared once every seven years — on the anniversary of her death.

Few traces of Gallagher's old neighbourhood remain in Montreal. Abandoned factories and slum housing have been replaced by film studios and trendy condos looking out over the Lachine Canal. But some folks still gather every seven years at the corner of William and Murray Streets to mark the passing of the lively, close-knit Irish-Canadian community that once was Griffintown. And they do so on June 27, just in case the headless ghost of Mary Gallagher decides to go for a walk that night.

A FINE HOME FOR A GHOST

Regina, Saskatchewan

It isn't only in Griffintown that people gather in the hopes of running into a ghost. Every October, groups of schoolchildren have looked forward to class tours of Saskatchewan's Government House — because it's said to be haunted.

Government House is a splendid mansion located in Regina's Exhibition Park. Built in the early 1890s, it was at first home to the lieutenant-governor of the Northwest Territories, and then to the lieutenant-governor of Saskatchewan, after that province joined Confederation in 1905. In 1945, when World War II ended, the federal government moved the lieutenant-governor to the Hotel Saskatchewan and used the government residence to care for wounded veterans who had returned from combat. Twelve years later, it became an adult education centre.

Government House, ca. 1940s

In the 1970s several groups interested in preserving Regina's historic sites organized an effort to restore the building to its original elegance, and in the 1980s it became Government House again. Lieutenant-governors didn't live in it anymore, but their offices have been there ever since, and it's where the Queen's representative hosts many special occasions. It's also home to a museum highlighting Saskatchewan's history.

The last lieutenant-governor to live in the mansion was Archibald McNab. He served the province in that position from 1936 to 1945. During that time a cook named Cheung became ill and died in his room in the servants' quarters. After his death people could still hear him shuffling around in his slippers through the house's many rooms. Some people still hear those footsteps.

The building's staff think it is Cheung's ghost that shifts things from one place to another, mysteriously opens and closes doors, flips up the corners of tablecloths, flushes toilets in empty bathrooms, and appears briefly in the kitchen every now and then. And even though it frightens some workers to feel an invisible presence hovering in the back stairwell, or to hear footsteps in the hall when they're alone, they've accepted the fact that a ghost has found a home in the mansion. They've even given him a nickname — Howie.

So Howie — whoever or whatever he is — gets blamed for all the strange goings-on in Government House. He's also the reason why youngsters are so willing to soak up a little history touring the stately home and museum. They're especially attracted by the program that runs in October. It's called "Halloween with Howie." It's fun, it's educational — and it sends shivers up their spines.

THE VOICE OF EVIL

Clarendon, Quebec

Susan Dagg liked her new log house. It was small — just one storey with an attic — but she, her husband, George, and their two young children, Susan and Johnny, were settling in nicely. They had built the home in 1889 on a farm at Clarendon, Quebec, a community on the Ottawa River about ten kilometres south of Shawville.

Imagine her disgust, then, when she returned from the cow barn after the morning milking to find her kitchen reeking of human feces. The filthy waste, most likely from the outhouse, had been smeared on the floor from one end of the house to the other. September 15, 1889, was turning out to be a very unpleasant day.

Two other children were living in the Dagg household at the time. One was Dinah Burden McLean, a poor eleven-year-old girl who had been sent from Scotland to an orphanage in Belleville — until a Canadian family came forward to give her a good home. The Daggs had adopted her with that in mind, and also in the hope that Dinah would help Mrs. Dagg care for the two younger children. The other was a second orphan, a boy named Dean who worked for various farmers in the area when they needed extra help.

Early on the morning of the 15th, Dean had found a five-dollar bill on the kitchen floor when he climbed down the ladder from his sleeping corner in the attic. In 1889, five dollars was a lot of money, and he had given the bill to Mr. Dagg, telling him where he had found it.

But George was suspicious. The night before, his wife had tucked that bill safely away in her dresser along with a two-dollar bill. After Dean headed outside to do some chores, George asked Susan to check the drawer to see if the two-dollar bill was still there. It wasn't. So George climbed up to the attic to look for it, and found it in Dean's bed.

Assuming that Dean was a thief, and that he had made the mess in the kitchen to distract them from the theft, the Daggs ordered him to leave and reported him to the local authorities. The next day, though, they weren't so sure they had done the right thing. Dean was gone, but the disgusting waste was back — in the cupboards, on the beds, and mixed in with the food supplies — and they had no clue who the nasty, filth-spreading culprit was. They had no idea, either, about who spilled milk, broke dishes, moved chairs, knocked over a table, and even splashed water in Mrs. Dagg's face.

Not only were the Daggs mystified about what was going on in their house — they were frightened. So when

George had to be away from home a few days later, he asked his father to come and stay at the house. That's how John Dagg ended up witnessing some of the spooky incidents plaguing his son's family. He was there when the windows started breaking. He went outside to try to catch the vandal but there was no one in sight.

To add to their misery, over the next several days the family had to put out dozens of small fires that broke out spontaneously — and one afternoon an invisible hand hacked off Dinah's long braid and cut out large chunks of young Johnny's hair. Then, just when the Daggs thought the situation couldn't get any worse, it did. The unseen force that had been tormenting them so terribly started targeting Dinah specifically. She began seeing a dark shape in the house when no one else could, and hearing a deep gravelly voice uttering shockingly crude and vulgar things. She was terrified, and so were the Daggs. Desperate for some peace, they sent Dinah to stay with John Dagg for a few days, and the haunting ceased. But as soon as Dinah returned, it resumed.

By then, word about what was happening at the Clarendon farm had spread throughout the district, and curious neighbours were showing up, hoping to see for themselves some of the eerie incidents. Desperate for an explanation, the Daggs consulted a fortune teller, brought in clergymen, and agreed to have a man named Percy Woodcock from Brockville, Ontario, spend some time with them investigating their plight.

Woodcock was a well-respected Canadian artist who was also very interested in paranormal, or supernatural, occurrences. Articles about the Clarendon spookiness in local Ottawa Valley newspapers had sparked his desire to learn more about it. He arrived at the Dagg farm on

November 16 and spent two days interviewing all family members and anyone else who had direct knowledge of the bizarre goings-on. He went outside with Dinah to a small shed where she had last seen the evil spirit that spoke to — and through — her. There he suffered through a stream of foul language and insults directed at him personally, including threats to break his neck if he didn't leave.

More encounters with the snarling, invisible speaker continued the next afternoon — when a crowd of neighbours gathered to watch Woodcock challenge the phantom to identify itself. In turn, it claimed to be both a devil and an angel, leaving observers frightened and confused. After Woodcock left, a minister arrived and the crowd started singing hymns. The ghoulish spirit joined in briefly, laughing at efforts to drive it away, and then it left, threatening to return the next day.

Woodcock kept detailed notes of everything that had happened at the Dagg farm in the fall of 1889. He also obtained signed statements from several other witnesses, and published his findings in a long report in a Brockville newspaper. He made no mention of the torment continuing after November 19, and there is no known record that it did. Why it ended suddenly after an agonizing two months, or why it began in the first place, has never been explained.

Some locals at the time thought the whole affair was a hoax. But why would the Daggs and Dinah try to fool people in such a way? What could they hope to gain, other than a lot of negative publicity? Besides, Woodcock made it very clear that he believed the Daggs and Dinah were sincere and truthful as well as confused and terrified.

There were some suggestions that a poltergeist might have been responsible for the bizarre events at Clarendon.

A poltergeist is said to be a mischievous, sometimes mean, spirit that does things like make strange noises, shake and rattle furniture and windows, snatch and grab small items, and send things flying around a room. It's usually active at night, and most often makes its presence known in a household that includes a teenaged girl who's under some emotional strain. After a few days or weeks, it seems to stop what it's doing as suddenly as it started.

A poltergeist haunting might very well explain what happened to the Daggs and Dinah. Maybe Dinah deeply missed her home in Scotland, leaving her vulnerable to an encounter with a nasty spirit such as this one. But there's no record of a poltergeist ever speaking through a person the way the Clarendon ghost did, and the identity of the evil presence that possessed Dinah — and haunted her new home in Canada — remains a mystery to this day.

GiRL iN THE RiVER

Pain Court, Ontario

Pain Court is a village located on the Thames River near Chatham, Ontario. It was settled in the late 1700s by poor immigrants from the Detroit area of Michigan who moved onto Indigenous lands here. By the 1820s it had become one of the earliest French-speaking communities in southern Ontario. The village's historical significance is highlighted on a plaque put up by the Ontario Heritage Foundation in front of Pain Court's Church of the Immaculate Conception. What the plaque doesn't say is that the area is reported to have been haunted for the last hundred or so years by a ghost.

It's thought that this restless soul is the spirit of Mary Jacobs, a young woman who had fallen for a man named Alex Miller. Her parents weren't impressed with this young fellow; in fact, they were furious that their daughter was seeing him. But Mary was in love with Alex and, according to her parents, after a big argument with them, she ran off with him. Some days later, she turned up dead.

According to one version of the story, Mary's putrid body was found partially buried behind the barn on the family farm, showing signs of death by foul play. Another story claims it was first hidden on the property and then thrown into the Thames, where it was found floating downstream. Even though the body bore marks of a severe beating, local authorities decided Mary had committed suicide by drowning herself.

Publicly, Mary's parents blamed Alex for her death, but privately they knew that he'd had nothing to do with it. Apparently, during the fight with their daughter over her choice of boyfriend, Mrs. Jacobs had flown into a rage and had beaten her daughter to death with a heavy iron. Then the couple had tried to cover up the crime — and since Mary's death was ruled a suicide, it looks as if, officially, they succeeded.

Over the years, the phantom presence of a young woman has been seen at different places along the river near the spot where Mary's body was found. There was even one report years ago of a young minister, a Reverend Knight, being scared out of his wits when he saw a woman's body floating in the river, only to have the vision suddenly disappear. Some local residents say it's Mary who haunts the Thames around Pain Court, looking for the young man she fell in love with. But maybe her spirit can't find peace because of the terrible way she died — at the hands of her own mother.

THE PHANTOM STEAMSHIP

Lake Superior, Ontario

For at least two hundred years, sailors worldwide have shared tales of seeing a ship called the *Flying Dutchman* — but they haven't all been talking about the same vessel. The original *Flying Dutchman* was probably a ship captained by a Dutchman named Hendrik van der Decken more than three hundred and fifty years ago. The ship never made it back to its home port of Amsterdam, Holland, and it was generally believed that it sank during a storm in the dangerous waters around the Cape of Good Hope at the southern tip of Africa.

But time and again, long after van der Decken's ship was lost, captains of other sailing ships reported seeing the doomed vessel and its ghostly crew. In some cases they even got close enough to the Dutchman's ship to hear him ask them to take some letters home. It was rumoured that any ship agreeing to take those letters from van der Decken would also be swallowed up by stormy seas. And so the legend of the *Flying Dutchman* was born, and lives on to this day.

Over time the "Flying Dutchman" tag came to mean any ghost ship fated to sail for all eternity the waters where it sank, and many different Flying Dutchmen are said to sail the world's seas and oceans. The mysterious fate of the steamship *Bannockburn* has earned it the spooky reputation of being the *Flying Dutchman* of Canada's largest, coldest and deepest Great Lake — Lake Superior.

The *Bannockburn* was a sturdy, all-steel steamer built in England in 1893 for the Montreal Transportation Company. At 74.7 metres, it was designed specifically to be just under the length restriction at the time for ships navigating the Great Lakes waterway. Any longer and they couldn't fit easily in the locks of the Welland Canal, which connects Lake Ontario and Lake Erie.

On November 20, 1902, the *Bannockburn* finished taking on a full load of wheat at Port Arthur, Ontario (now Thunder Bay). It was to deliver the wheat to the port at Midland, Ontario, on Lake Huron's Georgian Bay. Early the next morning it left Port Arthur and made for the open waters of Lake Superior. By late afternoon, despite a strong headwind, it was already nearly one hundred kilometres southeast of Passage Island. James McMaugh, captain of the *Algonquin*, a steamer sailing toward Port Arthur, spotted the *Bannockburn* and kept an eye on its progress for several minutes. At one point, though, he turned away briefly to deal with something that required his attention. When he looked back a minute or two later, he was surprised to find that he could no longer see the

Bannockburn. It was as if it had suddenly disappeared.

Assuming the steamer had been hidden behind a distant bank of fog, McMaugh sailed on, not worrying about what had happened until he heard later that the *Bannockburn* hadn't stopped in at Sault Ste. Marie as planned. In fact, after McMaugh's sighting, the *Bannockburn* was never seen again.

The waters of Lake Superior can be dangerous. Powerful storms often build up without warning, especially in the cold, wind-plagued month of November. After days of searching without success for the *Bannockburn*, everyone concluded that a deadly Lake Superior storm had claimed yet another ship and twenty-two more victims — the crew aboard the *Bannockburn*.

But starting in 1903, sailors on watch duty began to report seeing the *Bannockburn*, its running lights still working, churning through choppy waters toward Sault Ste. Marie. Other reports described the ship as being covered with ice, a ghostly white apparition sailing off into the darkness. And a few seamen even spoke in hushed tones of how they had seen skeleton-like crewmen with hollow eyes manning the ghost ship as it sailed silently by.

The Bannockburn downbound on the St. Mary's River between Lake Superior and Lake Huron in the summer of 1902

What happened to the *Bannockburn* — why it sank without warning, and where — is still a mystery. But it's not hard to see why the steamer has come to be known as the *Flying Dutchman* of Lake Superior, doomed to sail that Great Lake's waters for all eternity.

THE SHIP THAT WOULDN'T DIE

Arctic Ocean

Another sturdy steel cargo steamer, the *Baychimo*, also came to be known as a ghost ship, but not because it sank without a trace with all hands on board, only to reappear months or years later. In a way, the *Baychimo*'s fate was the exact opposite of the *Bannockburn*'s in that it seemed to be unsinkable, and ended up being dubbed "the ship that wouldn't die."

In 1969 a group of Inuit hunters reported seeing the *Baychimo* adrift in the Chukchi Sea, just west of Point Barrow, the northernmost tip of Alaska. Until then, everyone who knew about the cargo ship had assumed it had finally sunk. After all, the last time anyone had seen it was seven years before, in 1962, when some Inuit kayakers spotted it in the icy waters of the Beaufort Sea.

But people's assumptions about the fate of the *Baychimo* had been proven wrong before, so the fact that it was seen again didn't come as such a great surprise. What was, and still is, truly amazing is the fact that the *Baychimo* first disappeared way back in 1931.

The seventy-metre-long cargo ship had been built in Sweden in 1914. In 1919 the Hudson's Bay Company bought it and had it refitted. It had to be able to withstand the hazards it would encounter sailing the treacherous waters of the Arctic Ocean. In 1921 it was sent to the eastern Arctic to visit various HBC outposts on Baffin Island — where Inuit hunters came to trade furs in exchange for food and other essential supplies. In 1925 it was assigned to do the same thing along the western Arctic's shores.

In early July of 1931, with Captain John Cornwell at the helm and a crew of thirty-six on board, the *Baychimo* set sail from Vancouver on its regular annual trading run up the west coast of British Columbia, around Alaska, and through the Beaufort Sea to Victoria Island in the Arctic. But this trip would prove to be anything but regular. The outward-bound portion of the journey was going well, and the *Baychimo*'s hold was carrying nearly a full load of furs and skins when Captain Cornwall decided to cut short the trip after reaching Coppermine (now Kugluktuk) on September 5. He was worried because he was encountering more large ice floes than he expected to see at that time of the year. His fears were not unfounded. Disaster struck on the return voyage. That September winter came early to the Arctic, and on October 9, the ship found itself trapped in ice about one and a half kilometres from shore near Barrow, Alaska.

Via the ship's radio, Captain Cornwall arranged for

planes to pick up half the men as soon as weather permitted. Then he and sixteen remaining crew members began preparations to spend the winter with the steamer and its valuable cargo. The plan was to build a hut on shore, stocking it with supplies they hauled over the ice from the ship. They were also to store on shore as many of the fur bales as they could manage to move. And everything went according to plan at first.

All of the crew had moved into the large shack by the end of October and they were getting by fairly well, despite crowded conditions and the depressing lack of daylight at that time of year. The shack was actually warmer than the ship. But on November 24 gale-force winds and blinding snow began battering the shelter, and the men were forced to stay indoors for two days. On the morning of the 26th, when the storm had died down a little, they emerged from the hut to be greeted by an amazing sight. Snow and ice piled nearly six metres high had built up where the *Baychimo* had been trapped, and the ship was nowhere to be seen. Had the steamer been pushed underwater by that massive mountain of ice and snow? That's what most of the men thought, and the captain radioed HBC headquarters with the bad news.

But on December 3, Captain Cornwall received a message that shocked everyone. The *Baychimo* had been sighted about eighty kilometres north of their location, trapped in ice about eight kilometres off shore. A small group of Inuit and white trappers made several trips to the ship, taking away most things of value, including the remaining bales of furs. Those men reported that the steamer had a hole in its side, and would most likely sink as soon as the ice broke up.

Clearly then there was no longer any reason for

Captain Cornwall and his crew to spend the winter in their makeshift accommodations, and planes were finally able to reach them during the second week of February of 1932. They were all greatly relieved that the last voyage of the *Baychimo* had finally come to an end, with everyone returning home safely.

But while the voyage may have ended for the crew, it was far from over for their ship. It was almost as if, once freed from the control of human hands, the *Baychimo* had taken on a life of its own. Against all odds, it survived the next thaw, and many others afterward, and continued to sail the waters of the western Arctic. It was seen three times over the next two years, and again in 1935 and 1939. After World War II, researchers and explorers joined Inuit kayakers and dog-sledders in reporting they had seen "the ship that wouldn't die." Looking ever more rusty and battered as time passed, it still managed to survive decades of brutal Arctic winters and to continue on its mysterious voyage to some unknown destination, dodging deadly icebergs along the way.

The Baychimo *lies high and dry on ice, 2.4 km from Barrow, Alaska, 1933.*

It's been nearly forty years since the Inuit hunters reported seeing the *Baychimo* afloat back in 1969. Surely it must have sunk by now. But who knows? People have believed that many times before, and over and over the sturdy steel steamer proved them wrong. Maybe it really is a ship that will never die.

THE INVISIBLE BEAST

Moser River, Nova Scotia

Moser River is a small village on Nova Scotia's coastal Highway 7, just west of the Halifax-Guysborough county line. The village takes its name from the river on which it was built, and both were named after Henry Moser. He bought land and settled in the area in the late 1700s.

Life in Moser River during the first half of the twentieth century was still pretty much as quiet and slow-paced as it had been for Moser's children and grandchildren. People made a living fishing, farming and working in the lumber business. Spending time with neighbours singing, playing the fiddle, step-dancing or playing cards was a pleasant break from the demands of work and daily chores.

Back in the early 1900s Bob Lowe, a Moser River resident, had just spent an enjoyable evening like that the night he got the fright of his life. It was raining when he left his neighbour's house, so he pulled up his coat collar and set out along the road toward home. Suddenly, out of nowhere, he heard a scrambling noise in the bushes. Then something unseen rammed into him, pulling off his coat and knocking him down as it raced past.

Lowe picked himself up, reached down for his muddy coat and, after a quick look around, ran home as fast as his trembling legs could take him. But even though he was scared, he was also curious about what had happened, so when he calmed down he went back out to the road armed with a rifle and a lantern. When he reached the spot where he had been attacked, he carefully examined the muddy ground and nearby bushes along the roadside. But try as he might, he couldn't find a single trace of who or what had struck him. All he could see were his own footprints. Then he heard the noise again.

This time Lowe could make out the sounds of a four-footed creature moving quickly toward him, but once again he could see nothing. He shouted into the darkness, hoping to scare off the invisible beast, but it kept coming. Once again Lowe started running as fast as he could. The phantom pursued him relentlessly until he neared home. Then its sounds suddenly faded into the darkness, leaving behind no evidence at all of its horrifying presence. But traces of the spooky run-in on the road near Moser River would remain burned in Lowe's memory until the day he died.

THE GHOSTS OF WAR

Fort Erie, Ontario

Each summer crowds of visitors take in the sights and sounds of battle re-enactments at the "Old Fort" in Fort Erie, Ontario. And every now and then a few of them have an unsettling encounter with a ghost from the distant past.

On the Lake Erie shore near the international Peace Bridge to Buffalo, New York, the fort played an important role in the War of 1812. The British army first built a small fort there in 1764 and used it to stockpile supplies during the American Revolution in the late 1770s and early 1780s. But in 1799 surging, ice-congested water flowed out of the lake into the Niagara River and washed most of the structure away. The same thing happened to its replacement in 1803, and the third, new-and-improved fort wasn't yet finished when the war between the Americans and the British, including Britain's Canadian colonies, began in 1812.

Troops stationed at Fort Erie at the time left it unfinished, taking supplies and weapons with them. The Americans took it over for a while in 1813, but abandoned it by the end of the year, when the British returned and resumed construction. The Americans captured it in July of 1814, and held off a major British attack that left more than one thousand British and Canadian soldiers dead. The British then laid siege to the fort and the Americans finally abandoned it for good in November of 1814, destroying much of it before leaving.

The Niagara Parks Commission restored Fort Erie in the late 1930s. During reconstruction, the remains of one hundred and fifty British and three American soldiers were found, and a monument was erected to mark their mass grave. Every August pretend "soldiers" stage the 1814 siege during which some of those men may have died. But could it be that the spirits of a few of the fort's former inhabitants may be taking their places among the actors?

One mysterious, uniformed soldier has appeared in the dining hall when no re-enactments were being staged, and another has been spotted hovering in a darkened corner of the fort. The bedding on an old bunk on display in the fort is often found rumpled and tossed as if someone has been sleeping there, and a shadowy woman — perhaps the ghost of an officer's wife — occasionally appears briefly in the sleeping quarters.

The lingering spirits of any number of individuals who died violently at the fort might account for such ghostly presences at the historic site, but it's the blood-chilling appearances of two specific soldiers that seem to have the strongest connections to Fort Erie's past. Some archeological evidence appears to back up old journal entries referring to what happened to these two unfortunate souls.

Back in the summer of 1814 an American sergeant named Benjamin White was getting a shave from another soldier when the room that the two men were in was hit by British cannon fire. White was decapitated and the barber's hands were blown off. Surely this story explains the scariest ghosts of all that haunt the fort — a soldier with no hands and one with no head.

Soldiers guard the inner gate at the entrance to Old Fort Erie.

GALLOPING GHOSTS

Bad Hills, Saskatchewan

Several years ago George Redhead, a farmer near Bickleigh in the Bad Hills region of Saskatchewan, had settled down for the night after a long day of plowing. He had camped out beside his truck so he'd be ready to get back to work as soon as the sun came up. Just as he was about to doze off, he heard the sound of a horse galloping toward him. He wondered who might be riding out there after dark, but didn't think too much about it until he realized that the hoof beats were getting louder and closer by the second.

Redhead began to panic. What if the rider didn't see his little campsite in the dark and rode right over him? He jumped up and moved forward, intending to wave off the unexpected visitor. But as his eyes adjusted to the moonlight, he was amazed to find there was no rider — and no horse — anywhere in sight. And yet the invisible horse kept coming until it swept past him and away, back into the still silence of the night. Dazed and bewildered, Redhead tried to settle back down, but sleep didn't come easily that night.

Years earlier, in 1932, two sisters from Bickleigh had a much quieter encounter with a ghostly galloper. At least they could see the wispy apparition that pounded toward them. But unlike George Redhead, Annie and Ivy Bristow couldn't hear a sound as the creature approached. In fact, it was the silence that frightened them most.

The Bristow sisters had been riding home in their horse-drawn sleigh when they noticed the phantom horse and rider loping along the train tracks. As the two women approached the point where the tracks crossed the road, their horses suddenly dug in, refusing to pull the sleigh any further until the spooky vision had passed. Only after it had raced off into the darkness did the sisters' team move. Then the two horses dashed off without waiting for a command, only slowing to a trot when they and the terrified travellers had reached the safety of the Bristows' lane.

In the 1850s and '60s, Métis from the White Horse Plains galloped across the Bad Hills, hunting buffalo. After Henry Wason, Bickleigh's first pioneer, settled in the area, other immigrants followed — riding horses to hunt, clear the land and visit neighbouring homesteads. Soldiers, fur traders, mail carriers, travelling preachers and schoolchildren also rode horses in and around Bickleigh well into the twentieth century. Was the ghostly rider the spirit of one of them? No one knows.

THE LADY IN RED

Toronto, Ontario

Toronto's subway system has two Bay Street stations — the one thousands of riders walk through every day, and another one below it that is closed to the public. Lower Bay, as it's known, was opened back in 1966 to help link the new east-west Bloor-Danforth to the existing north-south Yonge Street line. But after just six months, the Toronto Transit Commission decided it was better to keep the two lines separate, because when a train broke down on either line the entire system ground to a halt. So the stairs connecting the upper and lower Bay stations were blocked off, and the white-tiled lower station became a storage site for escalator parts and some maintenance equipment.

These days Lower Bay is often used by television and film crews shooting subway scenes. It's still used for storage too, and for testing new system signs and experimenting with possible changes to subway platforms. But a few TTC employees don't like being asked to spend time down there, especially not at night, because they don't want to meet up with the station's ghost.

The spectral "lady in red" drifts through the tunnel toward the station, occasionally moaning pitifully as she approaches. Wavy brown hair frames her face and falls across the shoulders of her long red dress. The apparition lasts just twenty to thirty seconds, but that's more than enough time for a frightened observer to see the dark hollows where her eyes should be. Even more disturbing is how she moves. She seems to have no legs — appearing to float just above the ground.

Is this lady in red the ghost of a victim of some terrible crime on the station platform, or of a tragic accident on the tracks below? No one knows. But it's easy to understand why a worker seeing her late at night wouldn't look forward to the possibility of encountering her ever again.

SPIRIT WALK

Toronto, Ontario

During the 1990s another Toronto location was a very popular choice for film and television producers, especially those who were trying to recreate scenes from the nineteenth century.

The area known as the Distillery District lies near Lake Ontario just east of Toronto's downtown core. It features some of the finest examples of brick and stone industrial buildings erected in the early to mid-1800s, and has been designated a national historic site. In the early 2000s, major restoration and renovations transformed the property into a contained, no-cars-allowed, village-like setting for boutiques, cafés, restaurants and art galleries. The new and improved Distillery District welcomed the public in 2003.

However, when it was used as a film set — and during its most recent transformation — ghostly goings-on at this place left some people feeling a little uncomfortable. Items moved mysteriously from one place to another, doors opened and shut on their own and strange sounds echoed from vacant nooks and crannies. One member of a television crew even reported seeing the spectre of a middle-aged man pass right through a closed door.

But some people say such unnerving incidents are nothing new, and that rumours of the Distillery District being haunted date much further back — to 1834. That was two years after James Worts, the original owner, built the first mill to grind grain on the site. Worts emigrated from England in 1831. The next year his brother-in-law, William Gooderham, joined him in Toronto and became his business partner. In time Wort's eldest son and Gooderham would go on to expand the milling business and build a distillery to process grain into whisky.

A view of The Distillery District

Unfortunately, Worts himself never lived to see the Gooderham and Worts Distillery Company become one of the most successful businesses in Toronto's history. In 1834 his world was shattered when his beloved wife died during childbirth. Twelve days later his body was found in a deep well on the property. No one knows for sure, but talk at the time suggested he was so depressed after his wife's death that he deliberately threw himself into the well. But whether it was suicide or an accident, Worts's tragic end seems to have marked the beginning of a series of eerie occurrences, leading to the belief that the Distillery District buildings are haunted by the ghost of James Worts himself.

But why would his ghost wander around the place? Does he have some unfinished business to attend to where he built the mill so long ago? Or is he still lingering near where he died, hoping to connect to the spirit of his beloved wife — so they can be reunited in death?

FRIGHT NIGHT

Victoria, British Columbia

The two Australian women camped out in the sprawling gardens of a vacant old mansion in Victoria in the early 1960s felt quite comfortable as they settled down for the night. They were experienced world travellers who didn't take foolish risks, and they had chosen their campsite with safety in mind. It couldn't be seen from the street and nobody else was hanging around the place. Besides, the price was right — it was free — and the view from the back end of the property — a rippling, moonlit tidal inlet known as the Gorge Waterway — was breathtaking. So they were totally unprepared for what happened a few hours after they fell asleep.

The shouting woke them both at the same time. Startled, they looked around. In the shadows they thought they could make out the dark figure of a small woman who kept shrieking at them to get out. They jumped up and started packing up their kits, anxious to move on. But suddenly the shouting stopped and they were alone again. Feeling confused and a little foolish, they took a few deep breaths to calm down, and then decided to stay where they were and try to get some more sleep. But neither of them got any more rest that night.

As soon as they slipped back into their sleeping bags the women were overcome by a sense of some invisible presence — a presence seething with hate because they were still there. They were exhausted and didn't want to move if they didn't have to, but the feeling of resentment became so unbearable that they finally packed up their belongings and nervously waited for dawn on the nearby bridge across the gorge. And as if they hadn't already been frightened enough that night, while sitting on the bridge their eyes became riveted on a mysterious red light that hovered in mid-air, moving back and forth just above the water below.

When a woman named Inez O'Reilly heard about the Australians' harrowing experience a few years later, she wasn't the least bit surprised. Learning where it had happened, she had no doubt that the women had had a run-in with her husband's grandmother, Caroline O'Reilly. Caroline would never have approved of the female travellers' unladylike behaviour. Ladies in her day wouldn't have dressed casually and would never have camped out on their own under the stars.

But Caroline's day was long gone. Nearly a hundred years earlier, in 1867, she and her husband, Peter O'Reilly, had moved into their new home on Pleasant Street, a fifteen-room mansion known as Point Ellice House. The garden of that house was the very place the Australian women had chosen for their campsite. By then, Caroline had been dead for more than sixty years.

Inez O'Reilly and her husband John moved into Point Ellice House soon after they married in 1965, and almost immediately Inez felt Caroline's presence in the place. The mansion had been neglected for a long time, and Inez and John felt compelled to restore it to its original grandeur. After two years of expensive and time-consuming effort, they opened Point Ellice House to the public.

But some visitors got to see more than the beautifully restored rooms and furnishings. They got to see Grandmother Caroline too. One child touring the house with her own grandmother left screaming because of her ghostly presence. Some people felt an invisible hand tap them on the shoulder. And one group on tour apparently spent nearly an hour with Caroline's daughter, Kathleen.

That happened on a day when Inez was so busy outdoors that she forgot about the group waiting to be shown around. When she finally realized her mistake she rushed back into the house, embarrassed and eager to apologize. But to her surprise, the visitors were preparing to leave, saying that the nice young woman in a blue dress had done a lovely job of conducting the tour.

Inez was stunned. Other than the tourists, she was the only one at the house that day. Curious, she took a few members of the group upstairs to Kathleen's room and pointed out a blue dress on display there. She asked if any of them recognized it. They all said they did, insisting that it was just like the one worn by the young woman who had given them the tour. Inez was convinced then that the ghost of her husband's Aunt Kathleen, who had lived in the house until her death in 1945, must have been the woman who ushered the guests through the place.

There have been other reports of appearances by Kathleen outside the house near the garden gate. Some people also believe that the ghost of Kathleen's brother, Frank, makes his presence known every now and then, speaking in a loud voice in what was once his bedroom. But Inez O'Reilly believed that because of the way she acted, it was Caroline, and no one else, who drove the Australian women from her garden more than forty years ago.

As for the mysterious red light that the two women saw hovering over the gorge, several people think they have an explanation for that eerie experience too. On May 26, 1896, the original bridge spanning the gorge collapsed, sending dozens of people aboard a tramcar plunging to a horrible death. The bodies of fifty-five men, women and children were recovered, but it was assumed that the death toll was even higher. Those who have seen the red light hovering above the water say it's the glow of a lantern carried by a spirit still looking for a loved one lost in the collapse.

Obviously, the Australians had no idea when they rolled out their sleeping bags that their chosen campsite was rumoured to be one of the most haunted locations in Victoria. If they had, that was the last place they would have chosen to spend their first night in the city, even if the price was right and the view breathtaking.

NOTES FROM NOWHERE

Winnipeg, Manitoba

Churches are seen as places of refuge, offering peace and comfort to all who enter. But the sudden arrival of a mysterious presence in a church can disturb its peace and trouble the souls of those present. Such an event took place at St. John's Anglican Cathedral in Winnipeg more than fifty years ago.

The cathedral stands across the street from St. John's Park, near the Redwood Avenue Bridge spanning the Red River. In 1817 Lord Selkirk set aside the land on which it is built for a church and a school to be used by the area's first European settlers, the Red River colonists. In 1822 a small mission church was constructed on part of what is now the cemetery. In 1833 a new, larger church was built where the current cathedral now stands, and a third one was erected in 1862. The existing church was built in 1926, using much of the stone from the previous two structures.

In 1927 a classic Casavant pipe organ was installed in the new church. Thirty-six years later that fine musical instrument would be the source of a very mysterious disturbance in the history-rich house of worship.

In December of 1953, a small group of parishioners gathered in the cathedral's chapel one Sunday afternoon to reflect on the meaning of Advent, a time when Christians prepare spiritually for the coming of Christmas. Reverend John Ogle Anderson, the rector or senior clergyman, was there, as was his assistant, a curate named Reverend H. J. Skynner.

Reverend Skynner had planned a very simple, informal service of scripture readings and prayer. But as he began his first reading, any plans for simplicity went right out the stained glass windows. Suddenly a single, flute-sounding organ note echoed through the building. Then another note. And another. No harmony was added, just single notes played slowly, one by one, with the flute stop pulled out.

The dozen or so parishioners present that afternoon were surprised to hear the strange melody interrupt the rector's reading. The organist wasn't known for making mistakes like that. But the rector and the dean were even more astonished. The organist wasn't there. And from where he was sitting in the chapel, Reverend Anderson could see that no one else was sitting in front of the instrument's two-tiered keyboard.

The haunting sounds continued to resonate throughout the cathedral for several minutes that afternoon. The next day the rector called in the technician who regularly serviced the organ, but the man could see nothing wrong with it. What's more, he found that all the stops, including the flute stop, were pushed in, preventing any wind from entering the pipes to make a sound. The organ had not been touched after the disturbingly strange episode and, set like that, it shouldn't have been able to make any sound at all. So the technician couldn't come up with any earthly explanation. Neither could the rector or the curate, and the identity of the invisible organ player with the ghostly tune remains a mystery to this day.

A HAUNTING MELODY

Edmonton, Alberta

A legend about another invisible organ player persists at the University of Alberta in Edmonton, but this phantom musician didn't play only one note, and didn't just play one time either.

Its instrument of choice was the War Memorial Organ installed after World War I in the university's original Convocation Hall. To honour individuals from the university who lost their lives during both the First and Second World Wars, their names are listed on plaques at the hall's entrance.

Perhaps the invisible organist also wanted to honour the war dead. It's rumoured that night after night, during World War II, the organ played "Taps" — the haunting twenty-four-note melody heard at American military funerals and memorial services and at informal Canadian services too. But there was no one to be seen anywhere near the keyboard when it did.

The pipes of the War Memorial Organ, 1941

A SPIRITED PERFORMANCE

Uptergrove, Ontario

By contrast, the ghostly organist at St. Columbkille's Church at Uptergrove, near Orillia, had no problem with being visible. He was even dressed for the occasion when he gave a brief recital in late March of 1964. More than forty years later, Susan Wallace could still clearly remember how he looked and how upset she was when she saw him.

Wallace and her two sisters were helping their mother and another woman clean the church just before Easter. Suddenly a mysterious, white-faced figure — all dressed in black and wearing a top hat — appeared in the choir loft. He sat down at the organ and began to play.

Worried that the stranger might be up to no good, her mother and the other woman climbed the stairs to ask him what he was doing there. When they reached the loft, he backed away without answering and entered the bell tower room, letting the door to it swing closed after him. The two women followed him, but were completely taken aback to find that the small, windowless room was empty. The door they had just come through was the only way in and out of the room, and the white-faced man hadn't gone past them. He had simply disappeared.

DINING WITH THE DEAD

Vancouver, British Columbia

Old buildings sometimes have strange tales to tell. The Century Inn and Bar, which opened in 2006, is an elegant restaurant on Richards Street near Pender Avenue in downtown Vancouver. It's located in Century House, a classic heritage building constructed in 1911 as a Canada Permanent Mortgage bank. After the bank closed in 1951, several other businesses set up shop there, including an insurance company, a trade school, a bookstore and another fine restaurant.

Sean Sherwood, the owner of the latest restaurant, personally supervised the restoration and remodelling of the building, but there were times when he felt some otherworldly spirit was also keeping a ghostly eye on what was happening. Occasionally when he was the only one in the place, he would hear mysterious laughter and haunting footsteps. He also got cell phone calls from what he believed was a female ghost.

What's more, a carpenter reported seeing a strange woman in old-fashioned clothes walking around the place. When he asked her to leave, she gave him such a scary look that he left instead, and wouldn't work in the building alone after that. Other workers also sensed the ghostly presence of a woman, and since the restaurant opened, some servers and diners have been disturbed by the sounds of a woman crying in an empty washroom stall.

Sherwood was aware of rumours that Century House was haunted when he finalized plans to open his new restaurant there. He'd heard the tale of how, decades ago, a female clerk was shot at the bank — either during a robbery or by her enraged husband. No one seems to have verified this story, but if it's true, could it be that the murdered woman's spirit is the otherworldly presence lingering in Century House?

THE PHANTOM TRAIN

Medicine Hat, Alberta

In 1908 Bob Twohey was working as a railway engineer on the Canadian Pacific Railway line in Alberta. He had a wife and children to support in Medicine Hat. One night in May he was in the cab of a train rolling along just south of there when a blinding light suddenly appeared in front of him. The closer it came, the more terrified Twohey became. Realizing that another locomotive was speeding toward him, he was about to shout to Gus Day, the fireman working with him, to jump. But at that moment the collision-bound train, its whistle blaring, swerved to the right and raced past his train into the darkness, its passengers waving from the windows.

Twohey had no idea what had just happened. A train couldn't possibly have passed his. There was just one track on that part of the line and his engine and cars were still on it. Figuring his imagination must have been playing tricks on him, he decided to say nothing to Day. However, he was troubled enough by the frightening experience that he asked to be allowed to do work around the railway yards for a while. It wasn't until a couple of weeks later that he screwed up the courage to talk to Day, and was both amazed and relieved to learn that Day had seen the phantom train too.

In June of that same year, Day was again working as a fireman aboard another train heading for Lethbridge. Jim Nicholson, a friend of Twohey's, was the engineer driving the train that night. And to Day's horror, in almost the exact same spot just a few kilometres outside Medicine Hat, the ghost train reappeared. Once again, its headlight grew brighter and its whistle sounded louder as it approached, and once again it swerved off just in time to avoid a deadly collision. Day said nothing to Nicholson about his second near-crash with a train that couldn't possibly exist, but he began to wonder if he, like Twohey, should take a break from the rails.

It was just by chance that Day was given a yard assignment in Medicine Hat on July 8, 1908. That's where he was when he and other workers got some terrible news about a derailment just a few kilometres outside town. A passenger train travelling east had been nearly two hours late leaving Lethbridge. This was a vital piece of information for the engineer driving a locomotive south to Dunmore Junction, to pick up the luxury cars of the Spokane Flyer. If he had paid attention to the Lethbridge train's new expected arrival time in Medicine Hat, he would have delayed his train's departure from the Hat. But somehow he missed that information, and his error proved deadly. The two locomotives met headlong, killing seven members of the trains' crews and two passengers.

When more details about the terrible accident reached the rail yards, Gus Day's mind was sent reeling, first with grief and then with horror. He was grief-stricken when he heard that the crash had claimed the lives of four of his fellow workers. Two had been good friends — Bob Twohey and Jim Nicholson. Twohey had been the engineer on the train from Lethbridge and Nicholson had been the other locomotive's engineer. Day was also horrified to learn that the crash had happened in the very same place as the two earlier encounters with the ghost train.

THE WOMAN AT THE WINDOW

Regina, Saskatchewan

The house at 1800 College Avenue in Regina is at the east end of a row of century-old buildings that the city would like to see preserved. But the house doesn't just capture the flavour of Regina's architectural past. If you believe many of the stories about the place, it also appears to have captured a spirit from the past — a ghost named Rose.

Over the years, there were reports of Rose being spotted looking out from windows and drifting along hallways upstairs. She was also blamed for turning lights on and off, and for mysteriously breaking into song. Back in the late 1990s, a man named Trevor Lein moved into the house. After three years, he converted his home into a popular spot called Magellan's Global Coffee House, which he ran for another three years.

During his six years in the building, Lein kept an eye out for Rose, but he never encountered her. No one in the Sneath family had met her either, and they had lived there from the 1920s to the 1980s. Lein found this out when he decided to investigate various stories about a woman dying in the house, and learned that they weren't true. No one drowned in a water tank on the property; it never had a cistern. A nanny rumoured to have killed herself by taking a dive out a third-floor window had, in reality, moved on to enjoy life in Calgary. And there had never been a serious fire in the house, so no one had burned to death there either — another possible explanation given for Rose's haunting presence.

But one worker at the coffee house didn't really care what the ghost's name was, or why it might call 1800 College Avenue home. All she knew was that she had seen it three times — a mysterious woman in a wedding dress. And once, much to her shock, the bride had walked past a window overlooking the street — a window *on the second floor.*

1800 College Avenue

Another staff member was upset when she was alone in the kitchen and the dough mixer turned itself on. And another woman waitressing there had an alarming story to tell. She was making her way toward the tables when someone began to move toward her. Closer and closer the person came — directly in her path — until it passed right through her. The terrified waitress reported what had happened, and then promptly quit her job, hurrying out of Magellan's without ever looking back.

By 2006 the building was home to a computer-related business, and no one was publicly reporting any eerie encounters there. But there are still a few people in Regina who scan the upper floors as they pass in front of 1800 College Avenue — just in case the spectre of a woman is looking down on them.

THE TALKING STATUE

Burlington, Ontario

An eighty-five-year-old bronze statue of a World War I soldier stands atop a granite cenotaph beside Burlington's
City Hall. The statue is similar to many others erected
across the country. Together with other monuments and
plaques bearing the names of members of Canada's war
dead, they are often the focus of special ceremonies held
each year on November 11 — Remembrance Day.

However, there were times when some of the people
who gathered near the Burlington statue to honour the
sacrifices of war found themselves paying more attention
to the statue than the ceremonies. But that's understandable. Who wouldn't be distracted by seeing a statue move
its hands or by hearing it speak?

Stories about the statue being haunted date back

to before the end of World War II. And the stories have followed it on its moves from Lakeside Park overlooking Burlington Bay to a traffic island on Lakeshore Boulevard and — after major additions to City Hall were completed in 1986 — to the new civic square on Brant Street.

Over the years, in each location, as people stood in silence around the statue on Remembrance Day, they reported hearing the sounds of sergeants giving orders and soldiers marching. Several times individuals heard one particular voice calling out, "My name is Alfred." That voice seemed to be coming from the statue. A few others heard the mysterious voice add, "I lived a hero and I died a hero." But perhaps most disturbing of all are the reports that the bronze soldier shifts his hands as he grips the

A ghostly mist surrounds the monument.

barrel of the rifle on which he leans, that his lips move and that, every now and then, he opens his eyes.

Among the names of the war dead listed on the Burlington cenotaph is that of Alfred Edward Johnson. Veterans Affairs Canada's records indicate that a soldier by that name died in action on August 19, 1942. Johnson, from Burlington, was one of one hundred and ninety-seven members of the Royal Hamilton Light Infantry brigade who were hit by German machine-gun fire as they stormed the main beach at Dieppe, France, on that date. His body, along with those of his brave comrades, is buried in the Dieppe Canadian War Cemetery far away in France.

Some local residents think that it is Johnson's ghost that haunts the statue on the civic square — and not just during memorial services. Rumour has it that the bronze soldier also moves at a time when many other spectres make appearances — under cover of darkness, at the midnight hour.

A GHOST IN THE AISLE

Calgary, Alberta

Years ago, a ghostly soldier similar to the bronze figure standing in Burlington's civic square made several appearances in Calgary — in the theatre at that city's Centennial Planetarium, now part of the Telus World of Science complex.

Sam, as the phantom came to be known, was dressed in the uniform of a World War I soldier. He would suddenly materialize in the theatre, walk around for a period of time, then quickly disappear as mysteriously as he had arrived. Staff and visitors alike reported seeing him, and some spoke of him following them for a few seconds. Others simply felt his presence as spots in the building became unusually chilly, and a few people smelled the scent of his shaving lotion.

It's been a long time since Sam was last spotted at the planetarium, but some of the staff who used to work there remember him fondly, and not with fear. However, a few other workers didn't wait around for the phantom soldier to stop making his spooky appearances. They bid him a not-so-fond farewell, quitting their jobs and finding employment elsewhere in a less scary, ghost-free environment.

THE PHANTOMS OF THE OPERA HOUSE

Orillia, Ontario

No one has seen the ghosts that haunt the Gordon Lightfoot Auditorium at the century-old Opera House in Orillia. Unlike Sam at the planetarium theatre in Calgary, these spirits prefer to remain invisible. But they don't remain silent.

One loves to play the grand piano. No one knows whether it's male or female — but every now and then, when the auditorium is empty, its haunting tunes fill the air. Its presence has frustrated technical staff who have heard the melodies — usually sad ones — drifting toward them as they work elsewhere in the building. No matter how quickly they rush into the auditorium to catch the piano-playing culprit, the music stops the instant they show up, and they never find anyone seated at the instrument on stage. A few workers have been upset enough by their encounters with the invisible keyboard player that they avoid being alone in the place, especially late at night, a time the phantom prefers for giving its performances.

There have been reports of other spooky spectres performing in the auditorium late at night. Again, the performers were invisible, but they definitely weren't quiet. A blast of cold air coming from the orchestra pit announced their presence, followed by the sounds of laughter, clapping, and shouts of "Bravo!" It's as if an invisible theatre troupe were taking a curtain call before a very appreciative audience. But there were no actors on stage, and the seats where the applauding audience should be were all empty.

The Orillia Opera House

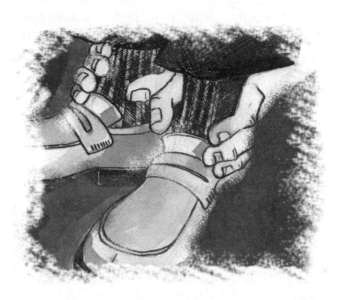

A GHOSTLY GUEST APPEARANCE

Georgetown, Prince Edward Island

The ghost who haunts another theatre, this time in Georgetown, P.E.I., doesn't mind being seen.

He inhabited the historic town hall — which became the Kings Theatre — before it suffered a serious fire in 1983. And he continued to reveal himself in the Kings Playhouse that rose from its ashes a few years later.

Like Sam, the Calgary ghost haunting the planetarium theatre, he's been given a name — Captain George. And he's a bit of a prankster. Wearing an old-fashioned military officer's greatcoat and carrying a lantern, he suddenly appears on stage or behind the scenes, leaving both crews and actors feeling more than a little uneasy. He's also been known to upset a few theatre-goers by briefly gripping their ankles.

Managers at the theatre finally decided to take a firm but friendly approach to dealing with Captain George. They reserved a seat specifically for him — hoping that he'd stay put in it instead of roaming around disturbing people, especially during performances.

If only he would . . .

DEATH AT THE MILL

Manotick, Ontario

Joseph Merrill Currier was a self-made man. Born in Vermont in 1820, he moved to the Ottawa Valley when he was seventeen, and found a job as a lower-level employee of a lumber company. Within a few years he had worked his way up to the position of manager of three different lumber firms, and by the late 1840s, he had earned a reputation around the Ottawa area as a savvy businessman. In the 1850s he and another successful lumberman, Moss Kent Dickinson, became partners, building a large sawmill and then a gristmill for grinding grain on the Rideau River at Manotick, Canada West.

But Currier's personal life didn't follow the same successful path. In 1855 scarlet fever claimed the lives of his children. Three years later, his wife, Christina, died. So he couldn't believe his good fortune when in 1860, while vacationing on Lake George in New York State, he met a beautiful young woman who seemed to be interested in him. Anne Crosby was half Currier's age, but that difference didn't stop the couple from falling in love, and they were married in January of 1861. After honeymooning in the United States for a month, Currier brought his bride back to Ottawa.

Currier was proud of his accomplishments. He was especially proud of the flour mill he and Dickinson had built at Manotick. Business was booming there, and a thriving village was taking shape around it. The mill had begun operating in 1860, and its first anniversary was coming up, so Currier thought a visit there would be a great way to introduce Anne to friends in the area and to show off the mill to her. However, early on in the couple's visit, tragedy struck.

Currier had walked Anne around the property, pointing out to her how water flowing over a dam on the river powered the machinery that turned the large stones grinding wheat into flour. Then it was time to tour the four-storey stone building itself. When they reached the second floor where the millstones were turning, Anne's long skirt and petticoat got caught in the revolving mechanism that drove the stones. In an instant she was thrown violently against a large support pillar, and slumped to the floor, bleeding. Horrified, Currier ran to her, but there was nothing he could do. His beautiful wife was dead.

Currier wanted nothing to do with the mill after that. He would never again enter the room where bloodstains from the horrifying accident remained permanently soaked into the wooden pillar, and he would never return to Manotick.

But it appears that his bride — or more specifically, her spirit — never left.

Over the years since Anne's death, several people have reported seeing a beautiful young woman in a long dress looking out of a second-floor window at the mill. Others have been frightened to hear blood-curdling screams coming from the mill at night when no one was there.

Watson's Mill, as it's now known, was bought and restored by the Rideau Valley Conservation Authority in the 1970s, and has become a popular tourist attraction. It's one of a few gristmills that are still operating in Ontario. But some visitors have felt very uncomfortable, especially when they are on the second floor. They start to shiver and feel cold there even on scorching hot summer days, and they have a sense that someone is watching them and wishes they would leave. Many believe that that someone is Anne — her spirit trapped forever where she met such a horrible fate. Perhaps she is wishing she could leave too.

Watson's Mill at night

Peace at Last

Joseph Currier married again, seven years after Anne died. His third wife was Hannah Wright, from Hull, Quebec. Hoping to start life afresh, he built a fine new home for Hannah, who came from a well-off family used to entertaining in a grand style.

The limestone mansion sat on a large tree-covered lot overlooking the Ottawa River. Currier called the place Gorffwysfa, a Welsh word meaning a peaceful place. He lived there until his death in 1884, and Hannah stayed on in Gorffwysfa until she died in 1901.

The stately house still stands in Ottawa, and Canadians like to think that the families who have lived there over the past many years have indeed found it to be a peaceful place. Its address? 24 Sussex Drive — the official home of Canada's prime ministers since 1951.

A DISTURBING GUEST

Winnipeg, Manitoba

The impressive-looking building at 335 Donald Street just north of Portage Avenue in Winnipeg was built in 1895. Known as the old Masonic Temple, it was the headquarters for local lodges, or branches, of the Masonic Order, a somewhat secretive men's organization whose members pledge loyalty to each other and support efforts to help others in the community.

In 1969, not long after the Masons sold it, the building became home to a Mother Tucker's Restaurant and, although the owner of the restaurant chain denied it, it was also home to a ghost. One server working there in August of 1979 actually saw the ghost for a few seconds. The apparition was that of a tall young man in a top hat and old-fashioned dress coat standing off to one side of the main room. But several other staff members who encountered the unusual restaurant guest usually just heard it or saw signs that it had been moving around the place.

After the restaurant closed, servers would tidy up and set the tables so they would be ready for the next day's customers. But some mornings when they returned, they would find serviettes wrinkled up, salt and pepper shakers knocked over, sugar spilt, and knives and forks lying in disarray. As one waiter put it, the dining room looked as if someone had had a party there in the middle of the night. Tom Sacco, the manager at the time, reported that he and others would occasionally hear mysterious footsteps moving around overhead, even though he had just done a security check of the upper floors before locking up. One night, sounds of a vicious argument were also heard coming from an empty room upstairs.

Generally speaking, though, staff at Mother Tucker's felt they could put up with the mysterious presence that seemed to prefer haunting the upper floors. They just did not want to be alone with it, especially not at night, after closing time.

A WRAITH ON THE WARD

Vancouver, British Columbia

At the time — back in the mid-1970s — officials at Vancouver General Hospital thought it would be best if the public didn't know the hospital's burn unit might be haunted. They were probably right. After all, knowing that a ghost could be helping out with their nursing care might not be such a comforting thought for most patients suffering from very serious burns. But if nurses were right about identifying him, the unit's ghost would have been very sympathetic toward their suffering. In life, he had himself spent three agonizing months bravely fighting to recover from horrible burns over much of his body.

The young man, referred to here as Jim — his real name was never publicly associated with the haunting — was one of sixteen workers seriously injured in a major explosion and fire in a grain elevator at the Burrard dock facilities in October 1975. Jim's injuries were the most serious. He was listed in critical condition and wasn't expected to survive. But, isolated in Room 415 to reduce the chance of infection, Jim somehow found the will to live and to cope with the excruciating pain caused by his third-degree burns. However, over the next several weeks his heroic battle sapped his strength, and three months after the fire he died.

Nurses who had cared for Jim were very sad when he died, but in the weeks and months following his death they began to think his spirit lived on in the burn unit, and not just in their tender memories of him. When some of them entered Room 415 to check on a patient, they began to feel that another invisible presence had entered with them. When nurse Denny Conrad was in the room one day getting it ready for the arrival of a new patient, he thought another staff member had followed him in carrying a tray of bandages. But when he turned around the tray fell, and there was no one else there. That incident disturbed Conrad; he didn't like the idea of being in the same room as a ghost, even if it was Jim's. Another nurse who went into 415 when no patient was there heard sounds of deep breathing coming from the empty bed, and saw the sheets move as if a patient were tossing and turning.

There were also reports of Jim visiting burn victims on the ward. One critically ill woman mentioned she'd just had a visit from a kindly young man she didn't know. The nurse was surprised to hear this since, as with Jim, the woman was being kept in isolation and was only allowed visits from members of her immediate family. Another time, a patient in Room 413 beside Jim's old room asked a nurse to pass along his thanks to the nice young doctor who had spent time with him the night before, helping him cope with his pain. The nurse was fairly certain no doctor had been on the ward then, but she checked the records to make sure and saw that she was right. Curious, she went back and asked the patient to describe what the doctor had looked like. She wasn't all that surprised when the patient described a man who looked just like Jim. However, she didn't tell the patient what she was thinking — that Jim's ghost had been making his rounds.

Most of the burn unit staff at the time felt that Jim's spirit was trying to be helpful when it actually made an appearance. Those occurrences were disturbing, but tolerable. However, some other ghostly activities were upsetting and even disruptive at times. Icy blasts of air would suddenly fill Room 415. Taps opened and the toilet flushed when the bathroom was empty, and the lights often switched on and off on their own. The signal to call for a nurse's assistance would also be triggered when no patient was in the room. Some people thought that these eerie encounters were Jim's way of letting them know he was still there.

Shortly before the burn unit was moved to another wing during the hospital's expansion, the unsettling incidents stopped. Nurses who had cared for Jim hoped that meant he had found pain-free rest at last.

THE DARK LADY

Hamilton, Ontario

The old Custom House at 51 Stuart Street in the north end of Hamilton is a magnificent stone building that is considered a national historic site. Opened in 1860, it was designed to look like many official buildings and museums constructed in Italy in the nineteenth century. It was built to house government workers who kept track of goods moving in and out of the city's busy port on Lake Ontario, and who collected duties, or special taxes, on many imported products.

Customs officials moved out in 1887 and, over the next hundred or so years, the building had many different owners and tenants. It became a temporary elementary school, a branch of the YWCA, a rooming house, a shelter for the homeless, several workplaces including factories that made vinegar, woollen yarn and pasta, a martial arts academy and a computer company. In the late 1980s the Ontario government spent a lot of money to help the karate school renovate and restore the building. In 1995 the current owner — the Ontario Workers Arts and Heritage Centre — bought it, using it to focus on the history and cultural contributions of Canadian working-class men and women. In 2001 the centre changed its name to the Workers Arts and Heritage Centre.

But while the owners and uses of the Custom House changed many times over the course of its colourful history, one thing stayed the same — the claim that the stately stone building was haunted by a ghost known as The Lady in Black, or The Dark Lady.

The Dark Lady is said to live in the basement of 51 Stuart Street, but she seems to move around a lot. There have been reported sightings of a beautiful woman appearing in a top-floor window of the building. However, a much older woman all dressed in black has also appeared in the place. In one instance decades ago, a worker named Mr. Hanman saw just the shadowy shape of a woman gliding along a wall. Years later, during the restoration, one member of the construction crew saw The Dark Lady clearly and got a sense that she was upset by the changes going on around her, especially plans to move the mantelpiece around one fireplace. Perhaps that's why she kept moving their tools after they went home for the day, and why she may have caused a major roof leak that flooded several rooms soon after the mantel was moved. Several workers also experienced a very strange, uncomfortable sensation and a blast of frigid air when they worked in the basement.

At least two stories offer a possible explanation for the tragic figure's lingering presence in the Custom House.

One says that she's the ghost of an unidentified immigrant who died on a ship that arrived in Hamilton and whose body was buried in the basement. Legend has her roaming the place for all these years as she waits for her lover to join her in Canada. Another tale that circulated years ago was about a ship's captain who murdered his wife and

A staircase leading to the basement of the Custom House

buried her there after she found out that he had a girl-friend and demanded that he end the affair. There seems to be no evidence backing up either possibility.

However, evidence that The Dark Lady has been around for a very long time may be found in a ballad by Hamiltonian Alexander Wingfield that was published in 1873. Titled "The Woman in Black," the poem begins with a specific reference to what the ghost wore.

The ghosts — long ago — used to dress in pure white,
Now they're got on a different track,
For the Hamilton Ghost seems to take a delight
To stroll 'round the city in black.

Wingfield then goes on to tell how frightened a police-man was when he suddenly encountered the black-garbed spectre while walking the beat near the Custom House one night.

A "Peeler," who met her, turned blue with affright
And in terror he clung to a post;
His hair (once a carroty red) has turned white,
Since the moment he looked on the ghost.

Wingfield ends the poem rather dramatically a few verses later, telling of how the poor officer was found frozen with fear at 2 a.m., still clinging to the lamppost. But according to another earlier verse, his terror was understandable. The apparition he saw was much more horrifying than the one usually seen at the Custom House.

Her breath seemed as hot as a furnace; besides,
It smelt strongly of sulphur and gin,
Two horns (a yard long) stuck straight out of her head,
And her hoofs made great clatter and din.

That ghost sounds absolutely demonic. Fortunately for those who've spotted the ghostly woman in black at 51 Stuart Street since that poem was published, the spectre they've seen doesn't smell of sulphur and gin, and she doesn't have horns or hoofs.

THE MAYBE GHOST

Orwell River, Prince Edward Island

James Hayden Fletcher didn't believe in ghosts. As a young boy growing up in a small community at the mouth of the Orwell River about twenty-five kilometres east of Charlottetown, P.E.I., he and his siblings loved hearing the spooky stories that workers at his father's sawmill would tell as they sat around the fireplace at the end of the day. The stories filled them all with a delicious mix of excitement and fear.

When he grew up, Fletcher was a little disappointed, but very relieved, to find out that most of those tales were grounded, not in facts, but in Irish and Scottish superstitions, and he stopped believing in ghosts. He even went so far as to try to convince friends and neighbours who did that they were foolish to do so.

Still, in an article titled "The Ghost Story" published in *The Prince Edward Island Magazine* in 1900 when he was about sixty, Fletcher admitted that those scary stories still had an impact on him as a non-believing adult. He confessed that "whenever I got into a suspicious place after dark, I always looked over my shoulder to make sure that no unnatural visitor was crawling on me from behind."

So it didn't come as a surprise that, as a young man, he started feeling very nervous walking home from the blacksmith's shop after dark one night, especially when he realized he would have to pass by an old graveyard. He tried to focus on the road ahead, but when he came to the cemetery gate, he couldn't resist turning toward it. He immediately wished he hadn't.

Decades later, Fletcher still remembered vividly what he saw that night — a mysterious, tall, white figure. In the "Ghost Story" article, he wrote about how he felt at that moment. "In spite of my philosophy, I felt my hat rise from my head . . . I looked out into the darkness again and saw it move! . . . There was no mistake about it — the spectre continued to move! . . . It slowly began to advance toward me. It gradually appeared to grow taller and whiter."

Fletcher was terrified, but he decided not to run, just in case the ghostly figure was the spirit of a close friend who wanted to communicate with him — a strange thought for someone who didn't believe in ghosts. Instead he decided to speak to it. "How do you do?" he asked, and was incredibly relieved to hear a human voice answer, "Well. Thank the Lord." Fletcher recalled, "It was the most welcome sound I ever heard, and yet I became so weak I could scarcely walk."

But walk Fletcher did, as quickly as he could, not lingering to chat with the white-robed figure, whom he thought he recognized as an old fellow from New Perth known as "Crazy Donald Gordon." Gordon had apparently become mentally ill in his old age, and had started wearing strange robes and performing bizarre religious rituals. Fletcher assumed Gordon had been saying prayers for the dead in the graveyard. Nevertheless, he readily admitted that nothing he had ever seen in his whole life had ever frightened him so badly as the appearance of the white-robed man in the cemetery.

But could Fletcher's first impression — that a ghost was moving toward him — have been correct? After all, he did mention in his article that Gordon had "scarcely ever been seen before in the vicinity of Orwell." He also referred to the man as a "patriarch," the head of a large family. A few old records point to the possibility that one Donald Gordon, who fathered many children, may have already been *dead* when Fletcher walked past the graveyard. Of course, records can be incorrect or incomplete. But maybe they weren't. Maybe Fletcher, the man who didn't believe in ghosts, had very good reason to be afraid that night.

PHOTO CREDITS

Pat Hancock

Pat Hancock's five Haunted Canada books combine spooky stories and eerie illustrations with interesting facts about Canadian history. Readers will be thrilled and chilled by her hair-raising stories! *Haunted Canada: True Ghost Stories* garnered the Saskatchewan Diamond Willow Award in 2004. A longtime collector of funny but true facts about Canada, Pat is also well-known for her four collections of Crazy Canadian Trivia books, now available in one volume as *The Big Book of Crazy Canadian Trivia*.

A former high school science and English teacher, Pat says that reading to her three children when she became a full-time parent first sparked her interest in writing. Now a grandmother of three, she still loves reading and writing both fiction and non-fiction for younger readers.

HAUNTED CANADA

Read the whole chilling series.

978-0-7791-1410-8

978-0-439-96122-6

978-0-439-93777-1

978-1-4431-2893-3

978-1-4431-3929-8

978-1-4431-4878-8

978-1-4431-8765-7

978-1-4431-4883-2

978-1-4431-4895-5

978-1-4431-7578-4

For Haunted Canada bonus material,
visit www.scholastic.ca/hauntedcanada.